CLASSICS OF WESTERN LITERATURE

Bloom County Books by Berke Breathed

Loose Tails

'Toons for Our Times

Penguin Dreams and Stranger Things

Bloom County Babylon:
Five Years of Basic Naughtiness

Billy and the Boingers Bootleg

Tales Too Ticklish to Tell

The Night of the Mary Kay Commandos

Happy Trails

Classics of Western Literature:
Bloom County 1986–1989

CLASSICS OF WESTERN LITERATURE

BLOOM COUNTY 1986–1989

Berke Breathed

LITTLE, BROWN AND COMPANY

Boston   Toronto   London

FIRST EDITION

Most of the strips in this book were originally syndicated by the Washington Post Writers Group.

Library of Congress Cataloging-in-Publication Data

Breathed, Berke.
    Classics of western literature: Bloom County, 1986–1989/
Berke Breathed.
        p.   cm.
    ISBN 0-316-10754-9
    I. Title.
PN6728.B57C5   1990
741.5′973—dc20   90-35829

10 9 8 7 6 5 4 3 2 1

RAI-BF

Published simultaneously in Canada by
Little, Brown & Company (Canada) Limited
PRINTED IN THE UNITED STATES OF AMERICA

FINAL WORD

Introductions for this kind of book are usually either cuddly testimonials by other cartoonists or nostalgic recitals of the author's childhood dreams of becoming a famous cartoonist. Here you will get neither.

It's not that it wouldn't make me feel all warm inside to have a pleasant testimonial from any of my colleagues; it's just that I can't think of anyone who would care to write one. Even if I could find a colleague who was fast and loose with flattery, or drunk, or preferably both, in return, at some later point, I'd have to write something knowing and nice for *his* or *her* book. That's the usual deal. And the problem is, I don't read the funny papers, and never have.

I can't recall ever asking Jesus to make me a comic stripper. I can't even remember reading *Pogo* or *Li'l Abner* or *Miss Peach*. I know of them now only because of a period of self-imposed postadolescent comics education that I undertook after suddenly finding myself in the business. Any proper comics education should happen no later than age seven.

As for me, at seven I was scanning the "News Capsules" section of the *Los Angeles Times*. Any headline including the words FIRE or MURDER promised something vital and was consumed by me no less voraciously than were the adventures of Dick Tracy by my future colleagues on other floors in other living rooms. Once, a caption reading "MURDEROUS FIRE" appeared below a photograph, and I knew then just how exciting and dangerous newspapers could be. *Hi and Lois*, on the other hand, pro-

vided no danger whatsoever, and therefore the comics page went unread. My father has since insisted that the funnies did indeed provide danger, of a sort, in the form of Daisy Mae's breasts. In the years to come I would understand this with a vengeance.

Drawing for humor didn't occur to me until I was in Mrs. Lewis's tenth-grade art class, in 1973 — specifically, just five minutes before I penned the lovely, museum-quality masterpiece reproduced here.

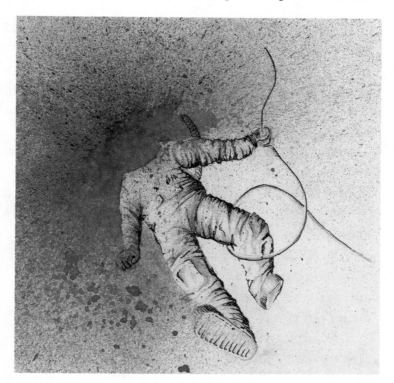

It's entitled *Gesundheit*. The special visual effects were created by my filling my mouth with red poster paint and blowing. Mrs. Lewis — ever gracious — displayed an expression of demure astonishment when I showed it to her, as if we were both at a White House dinner and I'd just farted. "It's awful. You're going to be rich," she said, and walked away. I had no idea what she meant.

I didn't draw another cartoon for four years. In 1977 I was hired part-time to draw political cartoons for the op-ed page of the *Austin American-Statesman*, and one of the first local issues thrown my way was a busing order imposed on the Austin school system by a federal judge. The populace got antsy. The paper's editorial board got cautious. My response, seen here, was a less than cautious parody of a familiar ad for the first *Star Trek* movie. The morning it appeared, the *Statesman*'s editor was hung in effigy on his front lawn. The effigy's papier-mâché head and a clipping of my cartoon were pierced with a toy arrow, a sort of shish-kebab tribute to the two of us. Later, the editor acknowledged the honor bestowed upon us by physically throwing me out of the building.

That event was a watershed. It steered me away from a career in political cartooning, a career that surely would have been highlighted by more butt-first exits from newspaper buildings. And more important, it revealed vividly that the public's emotional strings were within easy reach via a simple drawing and a word balloon. For me, at age nineteen, this revelation was like a siren song. I was hooked.

It should be clear from my confession of childhood comics illiteracy that I began my career with a numbing level of ignorance regarding the rich legacy and tradition of the American funnies. I say this not out of some perverse sense of iconoclastic pride but rather out of simple embarrassment.

It took me years to discover that the most important dynamic in a comic strip is not shock and satire, but character and truth: the truth of Charlie Brown's anxiety, for example — a mirror of our own. The truth of Calvin's protective manipulations of his world.

The truth of Opus's vanity and naïveté. To Charles Schulz and Bill Watterson, the secrets of truth and character surely must have come easily, as they stretched out absorbed on their living-room floors every Sunday afternoon of their youth, consuming the funnies as if they were rare confections. I, as you may recall, was busy looking for FIRE and MURDER.

This speaks volumes about why you can no longer find *Bloom County* in your daily newspaper. I have grown stubbornly affectionate toward my characters, and I have little desire to see Opus, Bill the Cat, and others disappear from my life. But after ten years of squeezing Bloom Countians into smudgy, postage-stamp-sized stories, I thought it might be more comfortable for all concerned if we took a powder from the daily pages. It is to be hoped that more expansive environments await.

Following this communiqué are cartoons from *The Academia Waltz*, a collegiate exercise in libel and nudity — a sort of compulsory rite of passage for most of today's comic-page artists. Out of the 658 strips that ran in the University of Texas's *Daily Texan* during 1978 and 1979, these sixteen are the ones that can probably be reprinted without my having to go to jail. In them you will see Steve Dallas in his inglorious gestational phase. The ugly fact is that he was admired — even worshiped — as a role model in some circles at the University of Texas. This was not my intent.

Cutter John (here called Saigon John) makes his first rolling entrance in these strips. Note that if the wheels on his chair were really as big as I've drawn them here, they'd be ripping clean through his armpits, leaving him armless as well as paralyzed. This is the sort of thing I notice now.

Here too can be found my early but growing fondness for outspoken animal life. Soon the little critters would dispense with the thought bubbles and converse openly with the humanoids. This sort of thing is anathema to most cartoonists, though I haven't the faintest idea why. I myself have made it a practice to talk to dogs and pigs in public, if for no other reason than that they seem to be listening — and until someone proves otherwise, they will talk in my cartoons. This is what happens when one doesn't have the familiarity one should with the traditions of one's profession.

Despite both *Doonesbury*'s omnipresent shadow and a dearth of penguins, I can see *Bloom County*'s stylistic signature struggling to emerge from *The Academia Waltz*. So these stale tarts from my past serve the same purpose as fading photos of ugly old dead relatives at a family reunion: in them you can see where all the goofy new characters in front of you came from.

Bon appétit....

FROM MY SKETCHBOOKS

Every idea — good or bad — started just like this. The tragedy is that pencil drawings never look quite as good once they've been civilized and transferred in ink onto the blank strip — a pity.

A BLOOM COUNTY SPECIAL REPORT...

LAWYER AND PART-TIME PHOTOGRAPHER STEVE DALLAS WAS ADMITTED TO THE ST. FERNHOTZ MEMORIAL HOSPITAL TODAY, SUFFERING FROM LOTS OF BRUISES AND A BROKEN BACK.. A RESULT OF AN APPARENT ASSAULT BY ACTOR SEAN PENN.

THE FOLLOWING BLURRY PHOTO, TAKEN BY THE VICTIM, APPEARS TO CAPTURE THE NEANDERTHAL THUG ONLY MOMENTS BEFORE TOTAL CHAOS BROKE OUT...

A REWARD OF $32.67 IS BEING OFFERED FOR THE PROMPT DELIVERY OF MOST ANY SUBSTANTIAL PORTION OF MR. PENN'S ANATOMY TO THE DESK OF MILO BLOOM AT THE "BLOOM BEACON."

MRS. PENN IS DISQUALIFIED FROM THIS OFFER.

MR. DALLAS... YOUR FRIENDS ARE HERE TO SEE YOU.

GROAN...

MY FRIENDS! OH GOD.. YES, MY FRIENDS! NOTHING BETTER TO LIFT THE SPIRITS OF A MAN IN PHYSICAL CRISIS THAN A SHOW OF LOYALTY BY HIS COMPADRES!

YOU'RE IT?

THEY'RE WATCHING PRO WRESTLING.

GAD...EVERY PORE OF MY BODY IS IN PAIN... EVERYTHING MUST BE BROKEN..

ONLY YOUR SPINE.

WHO ATTACKED ME? A MOB OF DRUG-CRAZED BIKERS?

SEAN PENN.

JEEZ...HE MUST'VE BLASTED ME WITH A 12-GAUGE.

HE POUNDED ON YOUR BACK.

WITH WHAT? A VOLKSWAGEN?

HIS FOREHEAD.

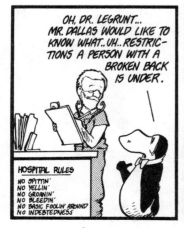

OH, DR. LEGRUNT... MR. DALLAS WOULD LIKE TO KNOW WHAT.. UH.. RESTRICTIONS A PERSON WITH A BROKEN BACK IS UNDER.

HOSPITAL RULES
NO SPITTIN'
NO YELLIN'
NO GROANIN'
NO BLEEDIN'
NO BASIC FOOLIN' AROUND
NO INDEBTEDNESS

JOGGING IS OUT. MOTORCYCLING IS OUT. DANCING IS OUT. SWIM--

WHAT ABOUT... ER...YOU KNOW...

HOSPITAL RULES
NO SPITTIN'
NO YELLIN'
NO GROANIN'
NO BLEEDIN'
NO BASIC FOOLIN' AROUND
NO INDEBTEDNESS

WHAT?

YOU KNOW...

WINK.. WINK WINK..

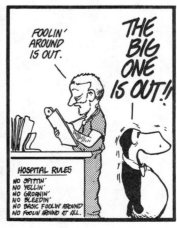

FOOLIN' AROUND IS OUT.

THE BIG ONE IS OUT!!

HOSPITAL RULES
NO SPITTIN'
NO YELLIN'
NO GROANIN'
NO BLEEDIN'
NO BASIC FOOLIN' AROUND
NO FOOLIN' AROUND AT ALL.

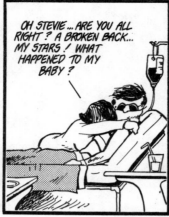

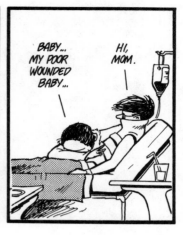

A CONFESSION, STEVE... I NO LONGER LOVE YOU. THE TRUTH IS THAT I WAS ONLY INTERESTED IN YOUR BODY.

MY BODY?

YOUR BODY.

JUST MY BODY?

YES. AND NOW IT'S BROKEN.

AND MY MIND?!

...IS CABBAGE.

WE INTERRUPT THE COMIC FOR A VITAL PUBLIC-SERVICE MESSAGE: IN AN EFFORT TO OFFSET THE ALARMING 13% DECREASE IN FREQUENCY OF LEE IACOCCA'S FACE ON TV, BOOKS AND MAGA-ZINES WITHIN THE LAST SIX DAYS, WE OFFER THE FOLLOWING:

MR. LIBERTY AT AGE 5

HIS IMMIGRANT MOTHER

IACOCCA: TOO MUCH IS NEVER ENOUGH.

WHEW! I WAS GOING INTO WITHDRAWAL...

AS A TRIBUTE TO LEE "MR. AMERICA" IACOCCA, WE HAVE A SPECIAL GUEST STAR...

"VALENTINE"... THE DANCING COCKROACH! TAKE IT AWAY!

AHEM...

A TRIBUTE

OH GIMME HYPE! PUBLICITY! GET DEM STRETCH MARKS OFF MISS LIBERTY! MOCHA! POLKA! PATRIOTIC TAPIOCA... DAT'S WHAT IS MY IACOCCA!

UNION BUSTING! PROFIT LUSTING! LITTLE PINTOS ALL COMBUSTING! APPLE PIE AND DIET COKE-A! DAT'S WHAT IS MY IACOCCA!!

WELL! THAT WAS SIMPLY--

...AWFUL.

SHWAK!

A TRIBUTE

IT WAS A WARM JUNE DAY WHEN OPUS FINALLY HEARD THE NEWS.

WHAT NEWS?

...THAT COLLEGE-EDUCATED PENGUINS WHO ARE STILL SINGLE AT AGE SIX HAVE ONLY A 3% CHANCE OF EVER GETTING MARRIED.

BUT I'M SIX!!

...THIS CAN'T BE! THIS CAN'T BE!! I'LL DIE AN OLD WATERFOWL MAID!! OH, I WISH I HADN'T HEARD THIS!!

ANY REGRETS?

YEAH. I REGRET THIS WASN'T ANOTHER DUMB IACOCCA EPISODE.

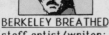

MAN OH MAN... I WISH THERE WAS A MILKSHAKE SITTIN' ON MY BELLY RIGHT NOW.

BLOOM COUNTY BACKSTAGE AREA
NO GROUPIES

MR. OPUS

SO ASK FOR ONE. WE'RE IN THE FUNNIES... ANYTHING IS POSSIBLE IN THE FUNNIES.

AWRIGHT. I'D LIKE A WHOPPING BIG SARDINE AND BEER MILKSHAKE.

BLOOM COUNTY BACKSTAGE AREA
NO GROUPIES

MR. OPUS

WHOA! THE COMIC WORLD REALLY IS A SEPARATE REALITY! I'D ALSO LIKE A PAIR OF RED SNEAKERS...

BLOOM CO. BACKSTA...

YOW! TOTALLY FAB! UH... NOW HOW 'BOUT A 200-POUND GREEN AND MAUVE DUCK SITTING ON MY HEAD...

BLOOM COUNTY BACKSTAGE AREA
NO GROUPIES

WOW! THE PHILOSOPHICAL IMPLICATIONS ARE STAGGERING! IMAGINE! OKAY... WHAT NEXT...

I'M OUTTA HERE.

MR. BLOOM

...KATHLEEN SULLIVAN... IN SPANDEX... IN A HOT TUB... FILLED WITH WARM JELL-O...

SO SORRY. LAST PANEL.

MR. OPUS

STEVE'S LAW TIPS

NUMBER 29
"WHO SHOULD I SUE?"

GOOD MORNING. TODAY'S TIP IS ON EFFECTIVE SUING. LET'S LOOK AT MY OWN RECENT EXAMPLE...

ON APRIL 17TH, THE PLAINTIFF, ME, WAS BRUTALLY ATTACKED BY ACTOR SEAN PENN AFTER I ACCIDENTALLY AND NOT ON PURPOSE SNAPPED A PICTURE OF HIM. THE QUESTION: WHO SHOULD I SUE?...

...SEAN?

NO. JURIES LOVE FAMOUS PEOPLE. PLUS, HE'D PROBABLY RETURN TO BEAT UP THE PLAINTIFF AGAIN. NEVER SUE PSYCHOPATHIC CELEBRITIES.

...SEAN'S WIFE?

NO. TRUE, LIVING WITH MADONNA MIGHT MAKE MOST ANYONE IRRITABLE, BUT PROVING LIABILITY WOULD BE DIFFICULT. PLUS, SHE TOO MIGHT RETURN TO BEAT UP THE PLAINTIFF.

...OPUS?

ME?!

...NO. ALTHOUGH HE GOT THE PLAINTIFF INTO THIS MESS, HE'S ALSO DEAD BROKE. NEVER, NEVER, NEVER SUE POOR PEOPLE.

...THE NIKOLTA CAMERA CO.?

NIKOLTA

YES! A MAJOR CORPORATION WITH GOBS OF LIQUID CASH, IT WAS CRIMINALLY NEGLIGENT IN NOT PUTTING STICKERS ON THEIR CAMERAS WHICH READ, "WARNING: PHYSICAL INJURY MAY RESULT FROM PHOTOGRAPHING PSYCHOPATHIC HOLLYWOOD HOTHEADS."

...I PLAN TO ASK FOR $10 MILLION...

AMERICA! LAND OF THE LAWSUIT!! GOD BLESS HER!!

Panel 1:
OPUS, BEFORE YOU GO OUT ON THIS BIG DATE, LET'S TALK... MAN TO FOWL.

RIGHT.

Panel 2:
SUPPLIES, ROMEO. AS A BACHELOR, ARE YOU FULLY PREPARED?... FOR ANY CONTINGENCY?

LESSEE... MONEY... VISA... ORGAN DONOR'S CARD...

Panel 3:
OPUS... DO I HAVE TO JUST BLURT IT OUT?

WHAT? WHAT?

Panel 4:
BREATH SPRAY.

OH YEAH, SURE! "SPARKLING SARDINE FLAVOR"!

Panel 5:
HELLO! YOU'RE THE LADY WHO CALLED ABOUT MY PERSONAL AD?

Panel 6:
YES. AND YOU'RE THE TALL, SVELTE, MUSCLED TOWER OF VIRILITY IT DESCRIBED?

YUP. SAY, THAT'S A REAL HEAD OF HAIR ON THOSE LEGS.. SO TO SPEAK.

Panel 7:
THANKS. YOUR NAME IS...?

OPUS. AND YOU ARE...?

Panel 8:
LOLA GRANOLA.

OF COURSE YOU ARE.

Panel 9:
WELL, MISS LOLA GRANOLA... NOW THAT WE'VE INTRODUCED OURSELVES, LET'S SKEEDADDLE ON TO THE RESTAURANT. TALLY-HO!!

Panel 10:
UH.. I'LL BE AT THE CAR IN A MINUTE, LOLA... I'VE LEFT SOME UNFINISHED BUSINESS...

Panel 11:
JUST THIS ONCE I'D LIKE TO BE ABLE TO GO OUT WITH A WOMAN AND POSSIBLE FUTURE WIFE WITHOUT ALL OF YOU TAGGING ALONG THANK YOU VERY MUCH!

Panel 12:
CLICK!

Panel 13:
WE INTERRUPT THE STORY TO READ A LETTER FROM THE EDWIN MEESE COMMISSION ON PORNOGRAPHY THAT WAS SENT TO ALL SIX AMERICAN NEWSPAPERS WHICH CARRY "BLOOM COUNTY."

Panel 14:
"DEAR NEWSPAPER EDITOR, WE HAVE RECEIVED TESTIMONY THAT YOUR COMIC PAGE INCLUDES A FEATURE WHICH FREQUENTLY MAKES USE OF THE 14-LETTER 'S' WORD..."

"THE 'S' WORD"?

Panel 15:
"THE MEESE COMMISSION HAS DETERMINED A CAUSAL RELATIONSHIP BETWEEN THE USE OF THE 'S' WORD AND THE RECENT INCREASE IN MURDER, UNCLE ABUSE AND DOG HICKEYS."

"THE 'S' WORD"?

Panel 16:
LADIES AND GENTLEMEN... I FEAR THEY ARE SPEAKING OF US.

"SNUGGLE-BUNNIES"?

..AND SUDDENLY MY F-20 FLAMES OUT AT 50,000 FEET... SPINNING WILDLY, I WRESTLE IT DOWN OVER THE FREEWAY AND SLIDE THAT BABY RIGHT IN ON TOP OF A SEMI FULL OF AVOCADOS.

DIDN'T SQUASH A ONE.

AND THAT WAS ALL BEFORE LUNCH TODAY.

SO. WHAT DO YOU DO?

I EAT HERRING HEADS AND LIE AMONG THE DANDELIONS THINKING HOW JETS AND AVOCADOS MAKE ME THROW THE HECK UP.

SAY, OPUS, PARDNER... WHADDYA SUPPOSE LOLA IS WHIPPING UP FOR DINNER TONIGHT? RAISIN BRAN? HA! HA!

I REMEMBER HOW SHE USED TO MAKE ME BREAKFAST IN BED... WHEAT OATMEAL! YUK! I'D COMPLAIN AND SHE'D SMEAR IT ALL OVER MY BARE CHEST...

HA! HA! HA! LOLA IS NO GREAT COOK... NO SIR!

..BUT BOY, SHE CAN KISS, CAN'T SHE?

I WOULDN'T KNOW.

SO HOW ARE YOU GETTING ALONG WITH BART?

SWIMMINGLY. I'VE BEEN HEARING ABOUT HIS ALLIGATOR-WRESTLING DAYS...

OPUS, I THINK YOU'RE JEALOUS.

DON'T BE SILLY.

YOU ARE.

AM NOT.

ANYWAY, DINNER'S READY.

I'LL GO FETCH "THE HUMAN CHIN."

UH-OH...LOOKS LIKE MY OL' PAL OPUS HAS HAD HIS CONFIDENCE SHAKEN IN THE ROMANTIC SELF-IMAGE DEPT..

WELL, C'MON... THINGS WILL SEEM BETTER TOMORROW... LET'S TUCK YOU SNUG INTO BED...

I'LL GET YOUR TEDDY BEAR... YOUR "GARFIELD" BLANKET... A PLATE OF "DING DONGS"... WHAT ELSE WOULD YOU LIKE?

A CHIN.

HOW 'BOUT SOME WARM MILK?

DAD... DAD, WE NEED TO HAVE A FATHER/SON CHAT.

DAD...YOUR BOY IS NOT GOING TO BECOME A STAR HALFBACK FOR THE DENVER BRONCOS. HE IS, HOWEVER, GOING TO BECOME A CAT.

DAD?... DID YOU HEAR ME?

MY JAGUAR XJ5 IS ORBITING PLUTO.

I KNOW, DAD, BUT WE'RE ON TO A NEW CRISIS. I NEED KITTY LITTER IN THE BATHTUB...

IT'S HAPPENED! OLIVER HAS COMPLETELY TURNED INTO A CAT!!

ACK! ACK! ACK! ACK!

AAIGH!!

HMM. I'M NOT A CAT AFTER ALL. IT WAS ALL JUST A HORRIBLE DREAM.

NOW, IF THIS WAS "THE TWILIGHT ZONE," THERE'D BE A STARTLING TWIST ENDING TO ALL THIS.

OLIVER, I HAD SOME TROUBLE WITH YOUR TELEPORTER THIS MORNING.

HERE IS THE INTREPID REPORTER FOR "THE BLOOM PICAYUNE" ON THE TRACK OF THE BIGGEST STORY OF HIS CAREER...

MILO'S WOODS DEAD AHEAD

..THE SEARCH FOR THE FABLED BASSELOPE! SIR... WHAT, EXACTLY, IS A BASSELOPE?

PART BASSET HOUND...PART ANTELOPE. VERY RARE.

A BASSELOPE SOUNDS VICIOUS. HAVE ANY PROTECTION?

BRINGING UP THE REAR.

THE SHOES ARE BY "REEBOK"... THE WEAPON, BY "LOUISVILLE SLUGGER"...THE FASHIONS BY "BANANA REPUBLIC." THANK YOU ALL SO MUCH!

YES, A BASSELOPE IS PART BASSET HOUND, PART ANTELOPE. THE MILITARY HAS BEEN LOOKING FOR ONE FOR YEARS...

APPARENTLY, THEY WANT TO USE THEM AS...UH... SAY...WHERE ARE YOUR NEW "BANANA REPUBLIC" CLOTHES?

TOOK 'EM OFF.

DO YOU HAVE ANY IDEA WHAT HAPPENS WHEN YOU HIKE UP A PAIR OF SHORTS AND YOUR LEGS ARE ONLY TWO INCHES LONG?

NO.

THE EXPRESSION IS CALLED "GETTING A WEDGIE," BUT I SHAN'T ELABORATE.

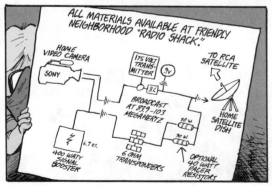

YEEEEAAH!

YEAH!! YEAH! YEAH! YEAH!

OO! OO! OO! OO! OO! OO!

THPTF! THPTTP! THPTH!!

ROCK! ROCK! ROCK! ROLL ROLL OLL

UH-OH.

CLAP! CLAP! CLAP! CLAP! CLAP! CLAP! CLAP! CLAP! CLAP! CLAP! MORE!

DISCOVERED AT LAST... THE FAMOUS ROCK 'N' ROLL AIR GUITARIST SLUMPS TO THE STAGE...HIS AIR GUITAR SPRAWLED ACROSS HIS CHEST. HE IS FATALLY EMBARRASSED.

SHOULD I LET THE AIR GROUPIES IN NOW?

WE'RE THE CREW OF THE STARCHAIR "ENTERPOOP" AND THE OFFICIAL BIRTHDAY COMMITTEE OF MILO'S MEADOW... AND WE'RE HERE TO BUY OUR GOOD FRIEND AND CAPTAIN, CUTTER JOHN, SOME NEW WHEELS!

HONEST SAM'S WHEELCHAIRS

SOMETHING SPECIAL AND DIFFERENT, PLEASE... DISTINCTIVE BUT NOT OVERBEARING... SINGULARLY UNORTHODOX WITH JUST A TAD OF FLASH! LIKE HIM!

LET ME SHOW YOU OUR TOP MODEL!

WHAT'S SO DISTINCTIVE ABOUT THIS?

MAUVE ARMRESTS!

DO MAUVE ARMRESTS MAKE A SUITABLE "PERSONAL STATEMENT"?

CERTAINLY NOT.

READ OUR LIPS... WE WANT SOMETHING DIFFERENT.!!

GENTLEMEN... A WHEELCHAIR IS NOT A VEHICLE FOR PERSONAL EXPRESSION!! PERIOD!!

SO HOW DO YA LIKE IT?

THE PHOTON TORPEDOES ARE UNDER THE REFRIGERATOR.

EAZ-E-BOY

WE MADE IT... DID YA GUESS?

DOES OPUS STILL THINK HE'S THE LATE MARLIN PERKINS?

I DON'T THINK SO...

YES, I THINK HE'S SNAPPING OUT OF IT.

THEY WANT ME TO WRESTLE WITH A TWENTY-FOOT ANACONDA!! PLEASE... TELL MUTUAL OF OMAHA "NO CAN DO!"

GET ME A BUCKET OF ICE WATER.

I'M 103 YEARS OLD... I HATE SNAKES!

The Bloom Picayune SCOOP!!
WORLD'S LAST BASSELOPE FOUND

FIRST BLURRY PHOTO

FOUND
"I SAW HIM PERSONALLY SLAUGHTER 63 WOMBATS AND DEVOUR A RHINOCEROS FOR BREAKFAST" REPORTS ACE REPORTER MILO BLOOM...

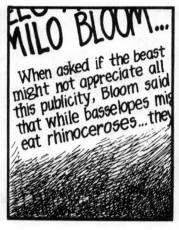

...MILO BLOOM...
When asked if the beast might not appreciate all this publicity, Bloom said that while basselopes might eat rhinoceroses...they

...they certainly don't read newspapers.

SO.. WORD WAS OUT... THE LAST BASSELOPE HAD BEEN FOUND. AND AMERICA'S ARMED FORCES MOBILIZED...LIKE THE ARMY...

THERE HE IS! SHOOT!

RUMMBBLE...

AND THE SPORTSMEN...

THERE HE IS! SHOOT!!

RUMMBBLE...

..., AND THE PRESS.

SHOOT! SHOOT!

RRUMMBBLLE...

REACTION WAS SWIFT...

IT'S THE MEDIA!! DUCK!!

GOOD MORNING. I'M MILO. YOU'RE VERY FAMOUS AT THE MOMENT AND I THOUGHT YOU MIGHT NEED A MANAGER. FIRST OFF... LET'S GET A SHORT "BIO" WRITTEN..

ROSEBUD
NO DISTURB-ING

OKAY... NAME AND FAVORITE FOOD...

"ROSEBUD." AND BASSELOPES LIKE "POP TARTS."

MARRIED? SWINGING SINGLE?

I'M THE LAST ONE. I HAVEN'T SEEN A FEMALE FOR 165 YEARS.

165 YEARS? HOW CAN YOU POSSIBLY--

BASSELOPES LIKE "POP TARTS" AND COLD SHOWERS.

OKAY...UH...HOW DID YOU ALL GET EXTINCT? NATURAL DISASTER? BUTCHERY BY MAN?

NOPE. NOPE.

I'VE GOT TO PUT IN SOMETHING INTERESTING... VENEREAL DISEASE? RECKLESS DRIVING?

CLOGGED ARTERIES.

CLOGGED ARTERIES?

BASSELOPES LIKE LOTS OF BUTTER ON THEIR "POP TARTS."

"Fast Living."

ROSEBUD, WE NEED TO FIND YOU A LITTLE ACTION.

DO NOT FEED THE BASSELOPE QUICHE

ACTION?

FEMININE ACTION. THERE'S GOT TO BE ANOTHER ONE OF YOUR SPECIES OUT THERE SUITABLE FOR SNUGGLING.

DO NOT FEED THE BASSELOPE PEACHES

DO NOT FEED THE BASSELOPE BOURBON

PERCHANCE, MIGHT MADONNA BE A BASSELOPE?

NOT THIS MONTH.

DO NOT FEED THE BASSELOPE OYSTERS

..SO WE'LL BE SIGNING THE CONTRACTS TOMORROW.

MY WORD.

..A MERCHANDISING DEAL TO PRODUCE PLUSH TOY BASSELOPES...

SOON I'LL BE SEEING THOUSANDS OF LITTLE STUFFED ME ALL OVER SHOPPING MALLS AROUND THE COUNTRY...

I'D PREFER TO BE PULLED OVER CARPET TACKS AND DIPPED IN RUBBING ALCOHOL.

IT'S NOT SO BAD. TRUST ME.

SON, WE WANT TO SEE THIS BASSELOPE THING. NOW.

WHAT FOR?

BASSELOPE REFUGE
BUG OFF

A SMALL TACTICAL WARHEAD WOULD FIT NEATLY BETWEEN HIS ANTLERS. IT COULD BE THE "MX" DEPLOYMENT SYSTEM WE'VE BEEN LOOKING FOR.

THE REDS ARE RUMORED TO HAVE A BASSELOPE. OUR SIDE HAS NONE. DO YOU KNOW WHAT THAT MEANS, BOY?

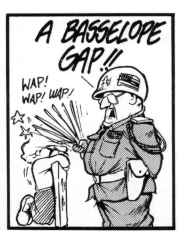

A BASSELOPE GAP!!

WAP! WAP! WAP!

WELCOME, FELLOW PROFIT-MINDED HEAD-BANGERS...

BAND AUDITIONS TODAY

I'M ONLY INTERESTED IN EXPERIENCED, DOWN 'N' DIRTY, GRIM 'N' GRIMY HEAVY-METAL MUSICIANS. NOW... UH--

IRON MAIDEN

YOU. FRONT AND CENTER.

HEAVY METAL? "WEIGHTY BRASS"... C'MON... GIMME A BREAK

AND NOW, MY RENDITION OF JUDAS PRIEST'S "SATAN LOVE BOOGIE"... THIRD VERSE... AHEM...

BAND AUDITIONS -QUIET-

LUCIFER, DO YER DUTY! SLAM MY HEAD, SHAKE YOUR BOOTY! WAM BAM, THANK YOU NELL, I'M ON THE AMTRAK TO HELL,

♫ BBLLAABTH! THPLAT! BWATT! THPROWT BBPPT!

YOU'RE IN, KID!

I WET MY PANTS.

"HELLO DARKNESS MY OLD FRIEND, COME TO SLEEP WITH ME AGAIN, WITH THE VISIONS SOFTLY--"

BAND AUDITIONS -QUIET-

I'M AFRAID "SIMON AND GARFUNKEL" ISN'T THE APPROACH WE'RE LOOKING FOR.

I'LL THROW IN SOME LEWD GESTURES.

I'M SORRY, ROSEBUD. NO.

LOOK... I BOUGHT SPANDEX TROUSERS...

NEXT!

OH, POOP!

CONGRATS, HODGE-PODGE... YOU'LL BE OUR DRUMMER.

OH, I'M SO HAPPY, SIR!

AUDITIONS QUIET METALLICA

BREAK THE BAD NEWS TO THE OTHER HOPEFULS. WHERE'S ROSEBUD?

REMOVING HIS SPANDEX.

AUDITIONS QUIET METALLICA

AAARGH...

I SMELL CATASTROPHE UPON THE WIND...

THAT'S JUST MY BREATH.

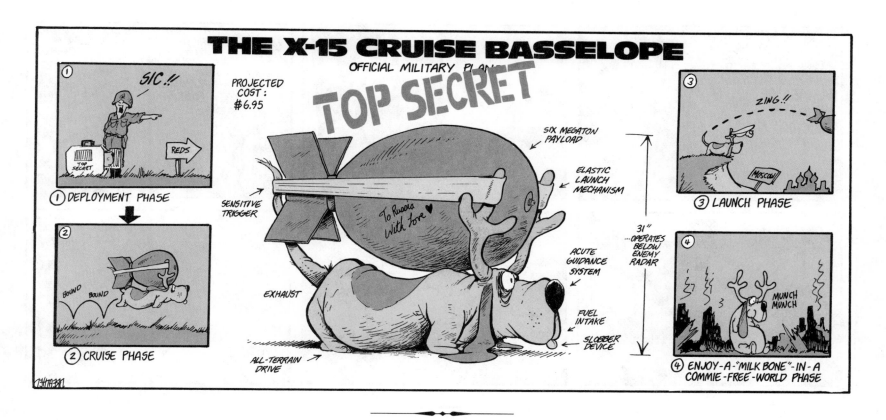

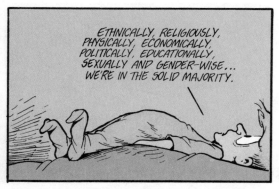

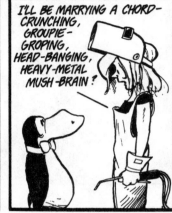

WHY DOESN'T YOUR MOTHER LIKE ME?

I DON'T KNOW. BUT REV. WILDMON DOES LIKE YOU. HE'S OUTSIDE TELLING HER RIGHT NOW.

SHE THINKS I MAKE TOO LITTLE MONEY.

NO, SHE DOESN'T.

I BELONG TO THE WRONG COUNTRY CLUB.

NO.

HE SITS IN THE FREEZER AND EATS FISH ENTRAILS.

NOW, LEONA...

WHERE'S STEVE, HODGE-PODGE?

IN LOS ANGELES WITH BILL, TRYING TO INTEREST A RECORD COMPANY.

INTEREST THEM IN WHAT?

THE MUSIC OF "DEATHTÖNGUE."

BUT THAT MUSIC GIVES PEOPLE INTESTINAL CRAMPS.

DON'T WORRY.. THEY'VE GOT AN ACE IN THE HOLE...

WELL, MR. CATT, WHEN STEVE HERE TELLS ME THAT YOU'RE PRONE TO BITING THE HEAD OFF A LIVE ROADIE ON STAGE, I SAY TO MYSELF, "CLIVE, THIS IS DAMNED EXCITING!"

NOW, BESIDES BITING THE HEADS OFF ROADIES -- WHICH I LIKE! -- WHAT ELSE IS YOUR ACT? ..THE VISUAL HOOK... GO ON... GIMME A SAMPLE...

BWONG BWONG BWANG..

SNAP! SNAP!

SAY! THIS IS GOOD! OH, THE KIDS WILL EAT THIS UP! WE'RE GONNA SELL RECORDS!

BLEACK! BLEAHCK!

YEAH! BLEAHCK! RIGHT!

BBBTHPT! BBTHBPT!!

PLATINUM! CERTIFIED! I GOT GOOSE BUMPS!!

I LIKE THE LOOK OF "DEATHTÖNGUE"... "MTV" MAGIC! BUT WHAT ABOUT THE MUSIC, STEVE BABY?

LEMME RECITE FROM OUR HOTTEST NUMBER... DIG THIS...

"MIDDLE-OF-THE-ROAD, MAN, IT STANKS LET'S RUN OVER LIONEL RICHIE WITH A TANK.."

WHADDYA THINK?

To Clive, Thanks! Lionel

YOU CAN SLAM THE DOOR BEHIND YOU.

THPPT.

SO THAT'S IT. I QUIT SMOKING... OR I KICK OFF IN SIX MONTHS.

YA MEAN CIGARETTES... ARE UNHEALTHY?

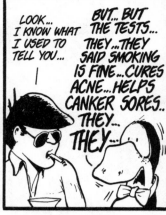

LOOK... I KNOW WHAT I USED TO TELL YOU...

BUT... BUT THE TESTS... THEY... THEY SAID SMOKING IS FINE... CURES ACNE... HELPS CANKER SORES... THEY... THEY...

OPUS!!

WHAT?

OL' BUDDY... THERE'S A CHANCE THE AMERICAN TOBACCO INSTITUTE'S HEALTH RESEARCH IS... WELL... BIASED.

GOOD LORD.

WHAT'S WITH BLOB-BUTT?

"IRANGATE" HAS OPUS A LITTLE SHAKEN...

AND THEN STEVE'S SMOKING-RELATED HEALTH PROBLEMS BLUNTLY EXPOSED THE HOMICIDAL HYPOCRISY OF AN ENTIRE INDUSTRY.

I THINK HE'S TRYING TO REACH A CONCLUSION REGARDING THE FAITH WE ALL LIKE TO HAVE IN OUR CORPORATE AND POLITICAL INSTITUTIONS...

NO, VIRGINIA, THERE REALLY ISN'T A SANTA CLAUS...

FELLOW "DEATHTÖNGUERS," I'D LIKE TO ANNOUNCE THAT I'LL BE TRYING TO QUIT SMOKING THIS WEEK.

IN FACT, I JUST NOW GAVE AWAY NEARLY EVERY SINGLE "MARLBORO" I OWN.

COUGH. GAG..

FRANKLY, I THINK THAT DESERVES SOME CONGRATULATIONS, DON'T YOU? HELLO?

CONGRATULATIONS.

THANKS.

BILL'S BAZOOKA-BARFING.

WHAT IN THE WORLD ARE YOU DOING, SIR?

HAZARDOUS DUTY. I'M GOING TO ASSIST MY GOOD FRIEND STEVE IN KICKING CIGARETTES COLD TURKEY.

AH. THANK YOU ALL FOR COMING OUT TO SEE ME OFF ON MY MISSION. WITH YOUR PRAYERS, I SHALL RETURN SAFELY.

HE'S... SO BRAVE!

THIS IS SO EMOTIONAL... :THPPT!:

IF ANYTHING SHOULD... UH, HAPPEN... I'LL SEE TO—

I KNOW. THANK YOU.

GOD... IS MY COPILOT.

GET IN HERE AND TIE ME UP, YOU IDIOT.

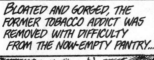

MEET DEATHTÖNGUZ

SECRET "DEVIL" SIGN

"WILD" BILL CATT
—SINGER / LEAD TONGUE—

HOLD TIGHT, HEADBANGERS...HERE COMES THE LOWEST, LOUDEST, LEWDEST BAD BOY OF METAL! AS THE TONGUE-STRUMMING, FRANTIC FÜHRER OF "DEATHTONGUE," HEAR HIM RAISE THE WIGS ON THEIR NEW ALBUM, "PIMPLES FROM HELL."

HODGE-PODGE
—DRUMS—

MASTER SKINS-BASHER HODGE LIVES FOR ONLY FOUR THINGS..."CHICKS, CHICKS, CHICKS" AND "DOUGH." BUT WHEN IT COMES TO DRUGS, THIS ROCK 'N' ROLL PARTY ANIMAL "JUST SAYS NO."

OPUS CROAKUS
—RHYTHM TUBA—

THE SHORT AND SEXY BOSS TUBA ROCKER OF "DEATHTONGUE" WANTS ALL HIS FANS TO KNOW THAT DESPITE THE LIPSTICK, HAIR, EYE MAKEUP AND PANTY HOSE, HE ISN'T A SISSY.

STEVE DALLAS
SONGWRITER / MANAGER

AS THE "BRAINS BEHIND THE SPANDEX," STEVE HAS PENNED SUCH PAST HITS AS "SKATEBOARDING TO SATAN," "GUILLOTINE YOUR PARENTS," "CLEARASIL MESSIAH" AND THE CLASSIC TEEN ANTHEM "LET'S ROLL OVER LIONEL RICHIE WITH A TANK."

ROSEBUD WAS HAVING ONE OF THOSE DAYS. IN AN UNEXPLAINED FIT OF OPTIMISM, HE TRIED A LEAP OVER THE FENCE ON HOOPER'S RIDGE. MILO FOUND HIM SOME HOURS LATER.

WHAT HAPPENED?

I'M HAVING ONE OF THOSE DAYS.

WORD SPREAD QUICKLY AND A CRISIS-MANAGEMENT TEAM WAS DISPATCHED..

WE NEED A CRANE.

LET'S BLAST 'IM OFFA THERE!!

LET'S NOT PANIC, GENTLEMEN..

CRISIS CONTROL

THINGS WERE TRIED...

PULL! OUCH! PULLING!

AND OTHER THINGS WERE TRIED..

PUSH! OOF! PUSHING!

ARGH..

BUT IN THE HARSH FACE OF FUTILITY, ALL THERE WAS LEFT TO DO WAS FIND THE LARGER MEANING IN THIS DEBACLE...

MEN... I SEE THIS WHOLE THING AS A METAPHOR FOR THE LIMITS OF U.S. POWER.

OF COURSE!

GREAT. LET'S GO HOME AND HAVE A "POP TART..."

AND SO.. AS THE LIVING SYMBOL OF AMERICA'S TROUBLED FOREIGN POLICY PRAYED FOR A LARGE SNOW DRIFT TO COME ALONG AND PROVIDE A DIGNIFIED ESCAPE, HE, TOO, REALIZED THAT BASSELOPES, LIKE NATIONS, SHOULD NEVER LET THEIR REACH EXCEED THEIR GRASP.

THE MORAL: I WANT A "POP TART."

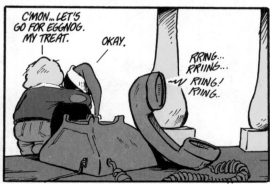

SOME OF US WERE WONDERING HOW YOUR ROMANCE WITH LOLA GRANOLA IS COMING ALONG.

WE WERE WATCHING A SYLVESTER STALLONE MOVIE LAST NIGHT AND SHE WAS SALIVATING.

YE OLDE PONDER PATCH

I ASKED HER IF **MY** BODY TURNED HER ON... AND DO YOU KNOW WHAT SHE SAID?

WHAT?

SHE SAID ALL SHE WANTS OUT OF A LOVER PHYSICALLY ARE "LIPS TO KISS AND A SHOULDER TO CRY ON."

THAT'S VERY SWEET.

I'M SHORT ON BOTH COUNTS..!!

YE OLDE PONDER PATCH

ARNOLD SCHWARTZENEGGER... MY GOD... THE MAN'S BODY IS... INHUMAN.

DON'T FOR A MINUTE THINK THAT I DON'T LOVE YOU EXACTLY THE WAY YOU ARE, HANDSOME.

IF I MAY MAKE AN ASIDE HERE, NOTE THAT MY "SIGNIFICANT OTHER" IS ON THE BRINK OF ENTERING THE CONVERSATIONAL ZONE OF A RELATIONSHIP THAT MANY OF US KNOW AS "THE BIG LIE." LISTEN.

PERSONALLY, I THINK THAT REALLY... HUGE MUSCLES ARE GROSS.

RIGHT.

"THE SCHWARTZENEGGER CHEST EXPANDER"... - INCREASE CHEST SIZE AND SEX APPEAL EXPONENTIALLY."

AARGH..

AAAIGH!!

BLOOM BOARDING HOUSE NO VACANCY

Local resident found unconscious with chest hair mysteriously ripped out

Police and medical experts are still trying to piece together the events surrounding yesterday's discovery of a small man who recently had all his chest hair violently torn out. He had apparently passed out from pain.

"Recovering nicely," said the vic... identify himself...

WELL! BACK AGAIN SO SOON, LI'L DUDE?

I, UH... WISH TO PURCHASE AN OFFICIAL "ARNOLD SCHWARTZENEGGER BARBELL SET."

Sears Sporting Goods

SO, THE "CHEST EXPANDER" DIDN'T DO THE TRICK, EH, DUDE?

SHH! SHH! SH!

Sears Sporting Goods

SIR... I WONDER IF WE MIGHT CONDUCT THIS TRANSACTION WITHOUT ALERTING HALF THE CIVILIZED WORLD IN THE PROCESS.

SURE. HEY, WHY THE CHEST BAND-AID, DUDE?

SHH!! SHHH! SHH!

Sears Sporting Goods

UNO...
DOS...

OOF!
UH OH...

BANG
BANG
BANG!
BANG
BANG
BANG!!

HOLY
MACKEREL...

RUN!!

THIS UNFORTUNATE AFFAIR WAS TO END SUDDENLY DOWN IN "MILLER'S MUD FLATS" WITH SOME INJURY. AND WHILE EVENTS WERE MARKED WITH GENERAL CHAOS, IT WAS, NEVERTHELESS, APPARENT TO ALL THAT THE "SCHWARTZENEGGERIZATION" OF OPUS WAS SIMPLY NOT TO BE.

BANG!

I'M ABOUT TO GO IN AND VISIT LOLA IN HER STUDIO...

HOWEVER, THERE'S ANOTHER ROMANTIC LAND MINE APPROACHING ON THE PATH OF OUR MATURING RELATIONSHIP...

COME ON IN, SWEET PEA!

..IT'S DANGEROUS... EVEN MORE POTENTIALLY CATASTROPHIC THAN "THE BIG LIE" FROM LAST WEEK!

I'M WORKING ON MY LATEST PAINTING...

HERE IT COMES... "THE HONEST OPINION"! YEEK!

TELL ME IF YOU THINK IT'S WONDERFUL.

HELLO, SUGARPLUM.

HI. REMEMBER HOW YOU SAID YOU'D NEVER, EVER, EVER LIE TO ME?

...WELL, I FINISHED A NEW PAINTING... I'M CALLING IT "SWAN SONATA IN BLUE." TAKE A LOOK!

WHAT DO YOU THINK? HONESTLY.

"THE HONEST OPINION". IT HAS DESTROYED BETTER MEN THAN I.

THE NEXT ROMANTIC LAND MINE ON OUR TOUR OF A MODERN, MATURING RELATIONSHIP IS RIGHT HERE. OR **NOT** HERE, ACTUALLY.

LOLA, WHY DID YOU TAKE MY CEREAL BOWL OUT OF THE FRIDGE?

BECAUSE IT'S TOTALLY RIDICULOUS THAT YOU KEEP IT THERE.

BUT I *LIKE* A COLD CEREAL BOWL... I'VE BEEN REFRIGERATING THEM EVER SINCE I WAS A LITTLE KID.

YOU PROBABLY USED TO WEAR THEM ON YOUR HEAD, TOO. C'MON, HONEY.

WE CALL THIS "THE BIG ADJUSTMENT."

I REORGANIZED YOUR RECORD COLLECTION TODAY. I TOSSED THE OLDER STUFF.

MR. DALLAS, I BELIEVE THIS IS ONE OF YOUR "DEATHTÖNGUE" SONGS. LET'S REVIEW IT TOGETHER.

"LEMME GRAZE INTO YOUR VELDT, LEMME STOMPLE YOUR ALBINO, LEMME NIBBLE ON YOUR BUDS, I'M YOUR... UH..."

..LOVE RHINO.

"LOVE RHINO."

OFF WITH HIS HEAD.

♪ TWANG! TWONG!

TAP TAP TAP

WELL, MR. DALLAS... WE'VE HEARD YOUR SMUT MASQUERADING AS SONGS...

...AND WE'VE HEARD HOW TEEN PROSTITUTION, PREGNANCY, DRUG USE, CULTS, RUNAWAYS, SUICIDE AND POOR HYGIENE ARE SWEEPING THIS NATION.

WE THOUGHT YOU MIGHT LIKE TO SHARE WITH THE COMMITTEE ANY PARTICULAR CAUSES YOU MIGHT SEE FOR THOSE LATTER PROBLEMS...

I DUNNO. MAYBE THE PROLIFERATION OF NARROW, SUFFOCATING ZEALOTRY MASQUERADING AS PARENTING IN THIS COUNTRY.

OFF WITH HIS HEAD.

WE CAN'T DO THAT, TIPPY!

AWRIGHT... AWRIGHT... I'LL CONCEDE THAT THE NAME "DEATHTÖNGUE" IS NOT PARTIC-ULARLY CONDUCIVE TO POSITIVE, CHRISTIAN, ALL-AMERICAN THOUGHT IN OUR NATION'S YOUTH...

WHICH... UH.. WHICH, OF COURSE, IS WHY WE CHANGED OUR NAME LAST WEEK TO...ER..TO...

..."BILLY AND THE BOINGERS."

"BOINGERS"? WHAT'S A "BOINGER"?

SOUNDS VAGUELY WHOLESOME.

STEVE'S CAVING IN !!

MILO !! DID YOU JUST SEE THE HORROR THEY SHOWED ON TV ?!

WHAT? WHAT?

STEVE JUST BUCKLED UNDER SENATE PRESSURE AND CHANGED "DEATHTÖNGUE'S" NAME TO "BILLY AND THE BOINGERS"! ON TV !!

OH. I THOUGHT THEY WERE SHOWING CROSS SECTIONS OF THE PRESIDENT'S BLADDER AGAIN.

NO, NO, NO...

...OR MORE GRAPHIC DIAGRAMS OF THE PRESIDENT'S PROSTATE.

FORGET IT.

YA KNOW, FOR MY MONEY, YOU NEVER CAN SEE TOO MUCH OF THAT SORT OF THING.

NOBODY GIVE ME ANY TROUBLE. "BILLY AND THE BOINGERS"?

IT WAS ALL I COULD THINK OF...

SOMEHOW, IT JUST DOESN'T CHALLENGE THE SENSIBILITIES OF THE TRADITIONAL ESTABLISHMENT.

SORRY. IT'S OFFICIAL NOW.

SAY... MAYBE "BOINGER" HAS SOME UGLY, UNSAVORY CONNOTATION WE HAVEN'T THOUGHT OF!

AWAY, KNAVES!

MIGHT IT BE A VAGUE SEXUAL EUPHEMISM?

NO, THAT'D BE "BILLY AND THE DIDDLERS."

LOLA... DO YOU THINK YOU COULD STAND BEING MARRIED TO A... "BOINGER"?

SURE.

I SUPPOSE IT BEATS BEING MARRIED TO A "DEATHTÖNGUER."

YES, BUT IT DOESN'T BEAT BEING MARRIED TO KEITH RICHARDS.

YOU KNOW, I HYPERVENTILATE WHEN YOU SAY THINGS LIKE THAT.

I'M SORRY.

AN AIR OF...DANGEROUS EXPECTATION HANGS HEAVY IN THE OFFICES OF THE MIGHTY "BLOOM PICAYUNE"...

IT WAS FINALLY TIME FOR A TRULY FRANK ARTICLE ON THE PUBLIC-HEALTH THREAT OF AIDS... AND CHIEF EDITOR ARMAND DIPTHONG KNEW THAT WHAT HIS READERS NEEDED WAS... BRUTALLY EXPLICIT SEXUAL ADVICE...

EASY...

COURAGE, BOSS... SLOW 'N' EASY... YOU CAN DO IT...

"DON'T FOOL AROUND!!"

TAP TAP TAP

TRY IT AGAIN, BOSS!

COPY BOY! COPY BOY!

HERE'S THE "AIDS AND PUBLIC HEALTH" STORY. I... I TRIED TO BE AS EXPLICIT AS POSSIBLE...

"IT'S WISE TO AVOID (THE 'I' WORD) OR (THE 'A' WORD) WITH (THE 'H' WORD) IN EITHER HIS OR HER (THE 'A' WORD II) AFTER (THE 'L' WORD) WITHOUT A BRAND-NAME ('C' WORD)."

AM I WAFFLING?

YOU'RE WAFFLING.

BOSS... I THINK TODAY'S **AIDS** STORY WAS TOO WISHY-WASHY, AS USUAL...

YOUR FREQUENT USE OF THE TERM "INTIMATE CONTACT" HAS LEFT SOME OF OUR READERS CONFUSED. I TRIED.

MRS. DILLWHIPPLE IS ON THE PHONE. AGAIN?

MRS. DILLWHIPPLE COULD WELL USE A LITTLE EXPLICITNESS IN HER LIFE. YES, MADAM, YOU MAY CONTINUE TO SAFELY KISS YOUR CAT "WOOGUMS" FULL ON THE LIPS...

ATTENTION, EVERYBODY! I HAVE JUST SUCCEEDED IN WRITING A SHOCKINGLY BLUNT STORY ON SEX AND PUBLIC HEALTH.

BRACE YOURSELVES. WE MAY WELL LOSE ALL 14 SUBSCRIPTIONS OF THE "LADIES' CHURCH MUFFIN CLUB."

BUT NO MATTER! EVEN AS I SPEAK, COPY BOY MILO IS FETCHING VARIOUS OFFENSIVE AND EMBARRASSING WORDS FROM OUR FORBIDDEN-WORD VAULT TO MAKE THIS STORY A REALITY!!

GOT 'EM!!

THE STORY ON SEX AND PUBLIC HEALTH APPEARED IN THE NEXT MORNING'S "PICAYUNE"... EXPLICIT, YET INFORMATIVE.

AS EXPECTED, THE ENTIRE MEMBERSHIP OF THE "LADIES' CHURCH MUFFIN CLUB" CANCELED THEIR SUBSCRIPTIONS. THE REPUBLIC, IN GENERAL, REMAINED STRONG, HOWEVER.

YES, MOST JUST TOOK THE OFFENSIVE WORDS AND EMBARRASSING ANATOMICAL REFERENCES FULLY IN STRIDE...

..OTHERS, OF A MORE SENSITIVE CONSTITUTION... DID NOT.

OH OH OH OH

WHAT ARE WE WATCHING TONIGHT? "L.A. LAW."

TOO MANY YUPPIES. LET'S WATCH "THE NEW LEAVE IT TO BEAVER." "MOONLIGHTING" IS ON.

BRUCE WILLIS MAKES ME ITCH. BALDING, CHERUBIC MEN TURN ME ON.

DON'T GET THE WRONG IDEA. WE ACTUALLY HAVE LOTS IN COMMON. IN FACT, WE SHARE A RAPTUROUS LUST FOR FLOUNDER-BRAINS PÂTÉ ON "TRISCUITS." YOU'VE BEEN SNIFFING "SCOPE" AGAIN, SWEETIE.

WATCH WHERE YOU'RE STEPPING!!

IT MAY NOT BE CUTE AND FURRY, BUT THAT SNAIL HAS THE SAME RIGHT TO LIVE OUT ITS LIFE AS A BABY HARP SEAL DOES.

WE EAT THEM, WE WEAR THEM...WE TORTURE THEM FOR SCIENCE...WE POISON THEM ON OUR CROPS...AND WE EVEN WALK ON THEM!!

WE'VE GOT TO TAKE ACTION ON THIS!!

SNAIL, I DON'T MUCH LIKE WHERE THIS IS ALL DRIFTING.

THEIR MURDEROUS FEET SUSPENDED SAFELY ABOVE THEIR UNSEEN BRETHREN IN THE SPRING GRASS BELOW, THE NON-MEAT-EATING, NON-PESTICIDE-TREATED-VEGETABLE-EATING, NON-ANIMAL-TESTED-MEDICINE-USING, NON-DAIRY-CONSUMING, STRICTLY COTTON-AND-POLYESTER-WEARING "CRITTER DEFENDERS" PONDER THE HAPPY FACT THAT THEY ARE FINALLY...TOTALLY...COMPLETELY COEXISTING IN PEACE WITH ALL LIFE ON THIS PLANET...

HOLD IT! WE'RE BREATHING AND MASSACRING MILLIONS OF GERMS!!

BINKLEY...EVERYBODY'S HUNGRY. COME ON DOWN. WE PROMISE TO KEEP THE EXPLOITATION OF ANY ANIMALS TO A MINIMUM.

NO! I WILL NOT ACCEPT THAT MORAL PURITY IS IMPOSSIBLE!!

BINKLEY, GOD SAYS THOU SHALT NOT KILL...BUT WE REGULARLY KILL IN GOD'S NAME. DESPITE WHAT THEY TELL YOU, THERE SIMPLY ARE NO MORAL ABSOLUTES IN A COMPLEX WORLD.

EXCEPT THAT I'M ABSOLUTELY STARVING FOR A PIZZA.

HECK, WE'LL HAVE 'EM HOLD THE ANCHOVIES.

I'VE CALLED YOU FELLOW "BOINGERS" TOGETHER FOR A SPECIAL ANNOUNCEMENT...

OUR FIRST TOUR IS ON! WE GOT CORPORATE SPONSORSHIP!!

YEA!!

THPPT.

WHO IS IT?! "COORS"? "BUD LIGHT"? LEMME GUESS!

"PEPSI"!

"DR. SCHOLL'S ODOR-EATERS."

THERE'LL BE NO COMIC TODAY, LADIES AND GENTLEMEN. "BLOOM COUNTY PRODUCTIONS" IS UNDER SUSPENSION.

THE N.A.C.P.* CONDUCTED SURPRISE DRUG TESTS ON OUR PLAYERS THIS MORNING... AND SOME NUT CAME UP POSITIVE...

* "NATIONAL ASSOCIATION OF COMIC PRODUCERS"

THE ENTIRELY UNCALLED—FOR DISCIPLINARY ACTION INCLUDES THE CANCELLATION OF TODAY'S PROFIT—-ER, PERFORMANCE.

IN THE MEANTIME, ALL CAST MEMBERS ARE CONFINED TO THE DRESSING ROOM UNTIL WE FIND OUT EXACTLY **WHO'S BEEN TAKING WHAT** AROUND HERE.!!

SLAM!

WAS IT YOU?

NO, IT WAS **NOT** ME.

WHOEVER IT WAS, WHAT'D THEY TAKE?

ANABOLIC STEROIDS, I HEAR.

EXCUSE ME... I WONDER IF—

HERE. TAKE THIS BEFORE WE GO ANY FURTHER.

WHAT IS IT?

MY SEXUAL HISTORY. NAMES, NUMBERS AND ADDRESSES ARE ALL UP TO DATE.

THANK YOU.

...AND IF YOU'LL PLEASE FILL OUT THESE FORMS DETAILING ALL YOUR PAST INTIMATE PHYSICAL CONTACTS WITHIN THE LAST FIVE YEARS...

I HAVEN'T HAD ANY.

NONE?

NONE WHATSOEVER?

NOPE. I'M QUITE THE PRUDE.

I'M INTO PRUDES!

ME TOO!

I SAW HIM FIRST!!

BOY! ALL THIS PAPERWORK, JUST FOR DIRECTIONS TO THE MEN'S ROOM!

DEEP IN THE BOWELS OF THE BLOOM BOARDING HOUSE, A DARING EXPERIMENT IS BEING CONDUCTED... A BOLD AND FRIGHTENING FORAY INTO THE DARKEST FORBIDDEN RECESSES OF THE HUMAN UNIVERSE....

NOW LET'S SAY HELLO TO MY LOVELY CO-HOST... VANNA WHITE! OH, VANNA!!

CLAP! CLAP! CLAP!

=HOOT!=

OUR DEFENDING CHAMPION, WALLY ICKSTEIN, IS BACK AND READY TO WIN. SPIN THE WHEEL, WALLY.

OKAY, PAT.

IS THERE AN "E"?

RIGHT YOU ARE. ONE. CAN YOU GUESS THE PHRASE, WALLY?

I'LL TAKE A WILD STAB AT IT...

"TEA CUP"?

RIGHT!

STOP THE EXPERIMENT!!

VEGETABLE MATTER, GENTLEMEN... WE HAVE VEGETABLE MATTER!!

MY GOODNESS...

HE'S AN EGGPLANT!

THANK GOD WE WEREN'T PLAYING JOAN RIVERS, OR HE'D BE A SALAD.

Editor's Note:

DUE TO OVERWHELMING READER REQUESTS, WE PRESENT THE FOLLOWING "REQUEST" SPECIAL:

ALL ABOUT POLO

...AN INTRODUCTION TO THE EXCITING SPORT THAT COMBINES THE THRILL OF CROQUET WITH THE SKILLS OF ROY ROGERS...

Ⓐ **SUITING UP:** HERE WE SEE THE GREAT POLO PLAYER PULLING ON HIS OSTRICH-LEATHER "SPATOS." THE GIRAFFE-BONE MALLET BESIDE HIM IS CALLED A "WONKER." HIS COLOGNE IS CALVIN KLEIN'S "OBSESSION."

OOF

Bloom County Polo Club NONMEMBERS WILL BE SHOT.

Ⓑ **THE POLO PONY:** SWIFT OF FOOT AND RIPPLED WITH MUSCLE, THE POLO PONY—LIKE GEORGE BUSH—IS A BREATHTAKING BEAST... AND THE POLO PLAYER'S MOST VALUABLE ASSET.

=WONKER=

WRAPPED FOR SAFETY

Ⓒ **PLAYING THE GAME:** WE HAVEN'T THE FOGGIEST AS TO WHAT THE OBJECT OF POLO IS, BUT IT SEEMS TO INVOLVE A GREAT DEAL OF GALLOPING ABOUT, SWINGING AT BALLS AND HORSE SWEAT.

HERE WE SEE DEMONSTRATED THE CLASSIC "PRINCE CHARLES TECHNIQUE"...

WHOOSH!!

ZING!

WHACK!!

Ⓓ **THE POST-MATCH WIND-DOWN WITH BLOODY MARYS AT THE CLUB POOL:**

I SAID I WAS SORRY. HERE. READ A "VANITY FAIR."

I TINK WE TOULD LOOK FOR MY NODE AGAIN.

UPCOMING "REQUEST" SPECIAL: "ALL ABOUT MICHAEL J. FOX'S PITUITARY PROBLEMS."

AWRIGHT, EVERYBODY... SETTLE DOWN... PARTY'S OVER!

LADIES..PLEASE COLLECT YOUR THINGS... HODGE-PODGE, GET OFF THE LAMP AND PUT OUT THE FIRE IN THE REFRIGERATOR.

BILL! PUT ALL THAT DOWN! BILL...GET AWAY FROM THE WINDOW...

DISPATCH... GIVE ME THAT ROOM NUMBER AGAIN.

DINETTE SET CLOSING IN AT 12 O'CLOCK...

AWRIGHT, YOU MOTEL-WRECKING CONSPIRATORS... BAIL ME OUTTA THIS SLIME HOLE...

YES! SURELY! OF COURSE! UH...

YOU ALL SURE ABOUT THIS?

YES! GO ON!

FIRST WE'D LIKE TO RENEGOTIATE OUR CONTRACTS.

ARGRRR...

IF THIS ISN'T A GOOD TIME, JUST SAY SO! WE'LL COME BACK IN A WEEK!

OKAY, SMART GUYS... I'VE REWRITTEN YOUR *#$#@ CONTRACTS...

I GET 2% OF THE RECORD ROYALTIES... YOU GET 98.

99.

FORGET IT.

GIVE OUR BEST TO YOUR CELLMATE, "ROLLO THE MAD-DOG RAPIST."

AWRIGHT. 99.

PLUS "DOVE BARS" EVERY BREAKFAST.

STEVE! WHERE ARE YOU GUYS? OUTSIDE OF TULSA? WHAT?... YOU'RE ALMOST BROKE?

YER HAVING TO DOUBLE UP IN THE MOTEL ROOMS, EH?

YOU SOUND A LITTLE DEPRESSED.

...APPARENTLY I'LL BE SHARING A WATERBED WITH ELEANOR ROOSEVELT HERE.

YOU WOUND ME, SIR.

BILL WRITES FROM L.A. THAT HE'S QUICKLY REACHING THE UPPER LIMITS OF PERSONAL STARDOM...

SAYS HIS ENTOURAGE IS NOW ALMOST THE SIZE OF EDDIE MURPHY'S.

WHAT'S AN ENTOURAGE?

I SAID MR. CAT WOULD LIKE A BURGER WITH RODENT-INTESTINE DRESSING. NOW.

RIGHT.

NOW.

I TOLD YOU, **NO AUTOGRAPHS!!**

ANOTHER DISPATCH HAS ARRIVED FROM TOP BOINGER BILL THE CAT, IN L.A....

NO OBSCENITIES OR SPITTING IN STUDIO

"DEAR FELLOW ROCKERS: 'BILLY AND THE BOINGERS' WILL NOW BE A CRITIC-PLEASING, SOCIALLY CONSCIOUS POP BAND WITH LEFTIST OVERTONES. SIGNED, YOUR LEADER, BILL."

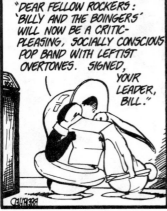

THUS THE BAND'S CHIEF LYRICIST SET OFF TO PURSUE THIS STARTLING NEW MUSICAL DIRECTION... ONLY TO DISCOVER WHAT GROUPS LIKE "U2" ALREADY KNOW:

..NOTHING RHYMES WITH "NICARAGUA."

..AGUA... BHAGWAN... OH, TO HECK WITH IT...

HE **WHAT?**

BILL WROTE FROM MALIBU AND ORDERED THE BOINGERS TO BECOME SOCIALLY CONSCIOUS.

A POLITICAL BAND? I'LL **KILL** HIM!

NOW, STEVE... I SUSPECT HE'S SUFFERING ENOUGH ALREADY.

WHY, JUST IMAGINE THE WRENCHING MORAL CRISIS THESE EARTHY, LEFTIST ROCK STARS LIKE BILL MUST FACE WHEN THEY BECOME FILTHY RICH.

HOW DO THEY DEAL WITH IT?

SNIFF.

SUPPORT THE HOMELESS

HODGE-PODGE! IT'S HERE! OUR REVIEW IN "TIME"!!

"WITH THEIR LATEST RECORD, THE NEWLY RELEVANT BOINGERS WEAVE TRANCE-LIKE MELODIES THAT SLIP OVER THE TRANSOM OF SOCIAL CONSCIOUSNESS AND INSINUATE THEMSELVES INTO YOUR DREAMS."

YEAH, BUT DO WE KICK BUTT?

READ IT AGAIN.

-YAWN- ANOTHER DAY... ANOTHER WEEK...

SOMETHING'S ON THE SCHEDULE BUT I JUST CAN'T PUT MY FINGER ON IT...

PAPER!

the Bloom Picayune

OPUS TO WED LOCAL WOMAN TUESDAY

HUNDREDS ASK: IS HE READY? DID HE RENT A TUX? DOES HE EVEN REMEMBER?

THANK *GOD* FOR THE AMERICAN PRESS!

I'M SUPPOSED TO MARRY LOLA GRANOLA TOMORROW AND I FORGOT?!

I, MYSELF, MARKED YOUR CALENDAR.

MILO.... HAVE YOU EVER HEARD AN ACTOR SAY HE'LL DREAM THAT HE WALKS OUT ON STAGE... AND CAN'T REMEMBER A SINGLE LINE?

YEAH.

SOUNDS DREADFUL, DOESN'T IT?

YEAH.

THIS IS WORSE!!

I'M NOT SURE HOW THE WEDDING SNUCK UP ON ME! THERE'RE STILL SO MANY QUESTIONS

LIKE.. WHAT ABOUT LOLA'S CAREER? WILL SHE WORK?

TRANSLATION: "WILL SHE HAVE THE TIME TO COOK AND CARE FOR ME?"

...DO WE WANT TO RAISE A FAMILY?

"DO I HAVE TO START ACTING MY AGE?"

AND FOR CRYING OUT LOUD... DO WE KNOW EACH OTHER WELL ENOUGH YET?

"WILL SHE DIVORCE ME AFTER SEEING HOW I LOOK AT SIX IN THE MORNING?"

THIS IS MOVING TOO FAST! I DON'T WANT A BACHELOR PARTY!!

YOU'LL HAVE A GREAT TIME. IT'S ALL SET UP IN THE STORM CELLAR.

OPEN UP! IT IS I... WITH THE DOOMED, SOON-TO-BE-ENSLAVED BACHELOR.. HERE FOR ONE LAST EVENING OF WILD AND LASCIVIOUS MALE REVELRY!!

DID YA GET WHAT I TOLD YA?

ALL WE COULD FIND WAS A 1964 "MARY POPPINS" OUTTAKE OF JULIE ANDREWS SAYING THE "S"-WORD.

THAT'S A STAG FILM?!

HEY...JUST THINK ABOUT IT! I GET GOOSE BUMPS!

IT'S TRUE. HE DOES.

I'D LIKE TO THANK YOU ALL FOR BOTH THIS PARTY AND THE GIFT OF THE ANATOMICALLY CORRECT LIFE-SIZE INFLATABLE DOLL. I'M TOUCHED.

YES, YOU'VE DONE SO WELL IN REMINDING ME OF ALL THOSE GREAT ASPECTS ABOUT THE SINGLE LIFE I'M LEAVING BEHIND:

LONELINESS... SELFISHNESS... TAWDRY ENCOUNTERS... V.D. ... AIDS... IMMATURE AND ANIMALISTIC ATTITUDES TOWARD WOMEN...

I'LL MISS IT ALL SO MUCH!

IS HE BEING SARCASTIC?

PARTY HARDY

WELL? DO I LOOK FETCHING?

I'D LIKE TO THINK MY ONLY DAUGHTER MIGHT WEAR MAKEUP ON HER WEDDING DAY.

NO GO, MA.

DEAR, I WANT YOU TO TAKE MY MAKEUP KIT... AND USE IT. TAKE THIS PHOTO, TOO.

A CLOSE-UP OF TAMMY FAE BAKKER?

I THOUGHT IT MIGHT HELP.

HELP WHAT? SCARE ROACHES?

WALTER, WOULD YOU TALK TO YOUR HEATHEN DAUGHTER?!

DEAR.. I THOUGHT THAT THIS SPECIAL DAY WOULD BE THE TIME TO DISCUSS... THE INTIMATE, PHYSICAL FACTS OF A RELATIONSHIP...

I'M 29, MA.

OH, I KNOW YOU'RE A LITTLE YOUNG FOR THIS...

I'VE KNOWN ABOUT IT ALL FOR ALMOST TWO DECADES, MA.

YOU WEREN'T SERIOUS, WERE YOU?

CATATONIC TRANCE

MA?

SO THAT'S IT, MA? THAT'S YOUR MAGIC FORMULA?

PATIENCE...UNDERSTANDING... PATIENCE... RESPECT... PATIENCE ... LOVE... AND MORE PATIENCE?

GOSH.. I ONLY HOPE OPUS IS GETTING SIMILARLY WISE ADVICE ON HOW TO KEEP A MARRIAGE ALIVE...

...SO THAT'S IT? HICKEYS AND BANANAS?

NO. I SAID SHE'LL GO BANANAS.

I'M... GETTING HITCHED TODAY!

THIS WAS TRUE. AND WITH A NERVOUS SYSTEM DULLED BY THE EXCESSES OF THE PREVIOUS NIGHT, OUR GROOM HEADED FOR HIS MATRIMONIAL DESTINY IN THE MEADOW...

WEDDING AHEAD

...STOPPING ONLY BRIEFLY FOR A FEW WORDS FROM THE BRIDE'S MOTHER.

WHISPER WHISPER

HOWEVER, THE BRIBE WAS INEFFECTIVE. **THE MARRIAGE WAS A GO!**

200! 275!

HELLO, LOLA. WELL... I GUESS THIS IS IT! THE BEGINNING OF THE GREAT ADVENTURE!

I'M SO HAPPY!

I COULD STILL RUN OFF TO BOLIVIA WITH A BIKER.

INTO THE ABYSS.

YOU LOOK HANDSOME.

YOU LOOK BEAUTIFUL.

SHE LOOKS BEAUTIFUL.

HE LOOKS LIKE A TOADSTOOL.

....I PRONOUNCE YOU WATERFOWL AND WIFE. YOU MAY KISS THE BRIDE.

KISS? BUT I'VE NEVER KISSED ANYONE BEFORE! I WAS SAVING MYSELF FOR MARRIAGE.

THIS IS IT, BUCKAROO. JUMP UP HERE AND PLANT 'EM.

.-WHICH, GENTLE READERS, OUR HERO **DID**. WHAT HAPPENED NEXT WOULD NOT ONLY AFFECT FUTURE EVENTS IN WAYS UNIMAGINED, BUT WOULD ALSO HIGHLIGHT A MARITAL PROBLEM HERETOFORE UNDISCOVERED...

...INCOMPATIBLE NOSES. LOLA WAS UNDAMAGED. THE GROOM, HOWEVER, WAS OUT COLD.

OW.

CONTINUED

IS HE DELIRIOUS?

YES. AND FROM WHAT HE'S MUMBLING...

..I'D SAY HE'S HALLUCINATING ABOUT MARRIED LIFE WITH YOU TWENTY YEARS IN THE FUTURE...

≥GROAN≤ ...COOK DINNER... CHANGE THE DIAPERS... CLEAN THE MICRO-LASER OVEN...

..NO, LOLA...FRANKLY, I **CAN'T** SAY THAT PRESIDENT STEINEM HAD A PARTICULARLY HELPFUL INFLUENCE ON THIS COUNTRY!!

WAAA!

WORLD'S BEST HOUSE-HUSBAND

MICRO LASER COOKER

THE WHOLE THING STARTED WHEN THE YOUNG INTERN AT THE "BLOOM PICAYUNE" ("CHRONICLE OF THE NEGLECTED TRUTH") SNIFFED OUT A HOT LEAD...

CUTTER JOHN IS PLANNING A SPECTACULAR DEMONSTRATION TODAY AT ELK'S HOLLOW. KEEP IT UNDER YOUR HAT...

HE DIDN'T.

I WANT PICTURES!! I WANT EMOTION! NO TELLING WHAT INSPIRING FEAT THIS DISABLED GUY HAS IN MIND!!

CITY DESK

NOT

HEADLINES WERE PREPARED FOR ANY CONTINGENCY...

"HANDICAPPED MAN PARACHUTES NUDE INTO PICKLE BARREL TO PROVE HE'S AS ABLE AS ANYONE"

GOOD. THAT SINGS.

CITY DESK

THE NEWS TEAM— SUCH AS IT WAS— SET OUT FOR THE RUMORED EVENT...

OKAY! THE MEDIA'S HERE! WHAT'S THE STUNT?

PRESS

TO ATTRACT HUGE NUMBERS OF FROGS BY MAKING LOUD VULGAR SOUNDS.

THBBT! FRRRT! THBPPT!!

THAT'S IT?! THAT'S INSPIRING?

IT WAS, ACTUALLY... BUT ONLY TO THE FROGGING INDUSTRY. BUT, NEVER ONE TO DISAPPOINT, CUTTER JOHN ATTEMPTED SEVERAL WHEELIES FOR INSPIRATIONAL EFFECT. ALAS, THE PRESS HAD LEFT, WHICH WAS JUST AS WELL, CONSIDERING THE QUALITY OF THE WHEELIES.

WHOA.

WHOA!

WATCH IT!

HE'S JUST GETTING WHAT HE DESERVES.

WHO?

GARY HART. I SAY NAIL THE DUDE.

WHY?

THE MAN'S GOT NO DISCRETION! I HOPE THEY THROW HIS BONES TO THOSE LEERING JACKALS OF THE PRESS!

STEVE... YOU'RE SO SEXY WHEN YOU'RE SELF-RIGHTEOUS...

SMOOCH!

SMACK

SMOOCH!

SMACK

THE CANDIDATE FOR THE ROTARY CLUB TREASURER RACE IS SQUEEZING MARY LOU MCDERP.

WHY, HE'LL BE SQUEEZING THE "CHARMIN" NEXT!!

BLOOM PICAYUNE SURVEILLANCE SQUAD

PRESS ASSISTANT

IT'S ALL IN ONE'S NAME, SOMEHOW...

..ONE'S DESTINY, I MEAN. EVER NOTICE HOW PEOPLE LIVE UP... OR **DOWN**...TO THE NAMES THEY'RE BORN WITH?

WOULD JOHN KENNEDY BE... *John Kennedy* ..IF HE'D BEEN BORN "MORTIMER DIPTHONG"?

WOULD FLORENCE NIGHTINGALE HAVE BEEN A HIT AS "LULU McADOO"?

ERNEST HEMINGWAY... MICK JAGGER... THOMAS JEFFERSON... THESE PEOPLE JUST WOULDN'T HAVE MADE IT AS "BIFF TURKLE".

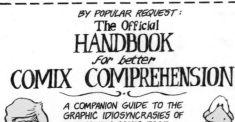
YEP. IT'S COSMICALLY ORDAINED. A GUY'S NAME CAN EITHER PROMOTE HIM... OR **DOOM** HIM. NO DOUBT ABOUT IT.

ME AND CASPAR WEINBERGER ARE GONNA **BEAT** THIS!!

BY POPULAR REQUEST:
The Official
HANDBOOK
for better
COMIX COMPREHENSION

A COMPANION GUIDE TO THE GRAPHIC IDIOSYNCRASIES OF THE MODERN COMIC PAGE ... AS ILLUSTRATED IN THE FOLLOWING COMIC SCENARIO PERFORMED BY MR. M. BLOOM AND MR. OPUS:

CLIP 'N' SAVE

I GOT AN IDEA!   WHAT?!

"BULBLE" [TRAD.] -SUDDEN INSPIRATION

"SURPRISLES" -SUDDEN MENTAL EXCITEMENT. POPULARIZED IN "MUTT AND JEFF," 1927-1939

"SWIVLES" -MOVEMENT, CHANGE IN DIRECTION. SEE "MOOVLES"

DON'T PUSH   NUCLEAR EXPLOSIVE

LET'S BLOW YOU INTO ORBIT!   HOLY MACKEREL!!

"MOOVLES" -MOVEMENT, PHYSICAL ACTION.

"SWEATLES" -ANXIETY, WORRY... ORIG. SEEN IN "POPEYE," 1929. MODERN USAGE RARE. STILL OCCAS. SEEN FLYING FROM HEADS OF CHARLIE BROWN, SLUGGO AND RONALD REAGAN

DON'T PUSH   NUCLEAR EXPLOSIVE

"ZIPPLES" -ACCELERATION. BASICALLY A LINEAR "MOOVLE"
ZIP!!
KABLAM!!

ZOOM!

"COMIC LICENSE" -HUMOROUS EXAGGERATION. FOR INSTANCE, A PENGUIN COULD NOT ACTUALLY SURVIVE THE LACK OF OXYGEN AFTER BEING BLOWN INTO THE STRATOSPHERE BY A NUCLEAR EXPLOSION.

SHOOP!!
"POOFLES" -SEVERE IMPACT. OFTEN IN ASSOC. WITH "STARS"
"SHOOPLES" -REVERSE "ZIPPLES"
WHAM!
"STARS" -SEVERE PAIN

THAT WAS GREAT!!
"BOOZLES" -INTOXICATION. IN THIS CASE, "ROOT BOOZLES"
"CRANIAL SMOKE" -BURNING HUMILIATION. CARCINOGENIC IF INHALED
AS CAN BE SEEN, WITHOUT PROPER FAMILIARITY WITH THE GRAPHIC SYMBOLS, A COMIC SEQUENCE SUCH AS THIS WOULD MAKE NO SENSE WHATSOEVER. LORD KNOWS, WE DON'T WANT THAT.

MARRIED LIFE IN 2007 A.D.

OH, LOLA? DEAR? WOULD YOU MIND IF I WENT WITH STEVE DALLAS AND HUNG OUT WITH THE GUYS AT THE CORNER COCAINE BAR?

NO! OUR 23RD CHILD IS DUE AT THE OSCAR MAYER SURROGATE TEST-TUBE EMBRYO FARM ... GO PICK HIM UP!

BOY... STEVE'S GONNA REALLY THINK I'M WHIPPED.

SORRY. CAN'T GO.

SHE'S GOT YOU WHIPPED, BLOBBO.

2007 A.D. ...

STEVE...YOU'RE STILL A BACHELOR AT 48 ... AM I MISSING ANYTHING?

NO SMOKIN ZONE

I MEAN.. AFTER TWENTY YEARS OF MARRIAGE TO LOLA, I'M SUFFOCATING!

NO SMOKIN ZONE

JEEZ! I GOT 23 GENETICALLY PURE, TUBE-GROWN KIDS! I NEED ADVICE!

ZBLAT!

YOU'RE THE LAST BUDDY I'VE GOT, STEVE!

DON'T FORGET TO CLEAN UP YOUR ASHES, SIR!

CIG POLICE

LOLA!! I'VE MADE A DECISION! AFTER TWENTY YEARS OF MARRIAGE, I NEED MY FREEDOM!! I NEED SOME ROOM! I...UH..

WAIT. HERE'S A NOTE FROM LOLA.

"DEAR OPUS, I'VE LEFT YOU FOR A ROCKET MECHANIC FROM TOLEDO. YOU CAN RAISE OUR 23 TUBE-GROWN KIDS."

WHO, ME?

YOU, POP!

...AN ABANDONED HUSBAND! ...MIDDLE-AGED! ALONE WITH 23 BABIES WHO LOOK VAGUELY LIKE HIM!!

"THIS IS A NIGHTMARE!!

AAIGGH!

AAIGH!

OPUS! WAKE UP! YOU'RE BACK AT YOUR WEDDING! WAKE UP!!

SAY SOMETHING, HONEY... ANYTHING!

ANNULMENT.

DAY THREE: "MEDIA HARASSMENT OF THE INNOCENTS AT HOME..."

HOLY MACKEREL.

MR. OPUS! MR. OPUS!

YOU'RE TRAMPLING MY PETUNIAS.

WHAT'S YOUR REACTION TO YOUR HEAVY-METAL COLLEAGUE GETTING CAUGHT IN A MORAL AND WHOLESOME SITUATION?

ER...WELL, ON ONE HAND, I'D OFFER MY LOYALTY AND SUPPORT TO MY HEAD-BANGER PARTNER AT THIS MOMENT OF CRISIS...

..ON THE OTHER, I'D LIKE TO DECK THAT STRAYING SON-OF-A-TULIP!!

DAY FOUR: "OLD PHOTOS SURFACE"...

DESPITE THE MEDIA'S LIES, MISS DROCK IS A FORMER MODEL AND OCCASIONAL ACTRESS. IN OTHER WORDS, SHE'S A BUBBLING CAULDRON OF WICKED LUSTFULNESS.

MY CLIENT WOULD NEVER RISK THE PEOPLE'S FAITH BY INVOLVING HIMSELF WITH A WOMAN ANY MORE RESPECTABLE THAN THAT.

SEE THE NEW "TIME"?

AAIGH!!

SISTER EDITH DROCK AT HER CALCUTTA ORPHANAGE IN 1982.

DAY FIVE: "THE FALL"...

IT'S OVER, BILL, OL' BUDDY... YOUR REPUTATION IS FATALLY BESMIRCHED WITH RESPECTABILITY.

YOUR CAREER WITH THE BOINGERS IS SHOT. PREPARE AN EMOTIONAL PRESS STATEMENT...

> SIGH <

..BE SURE TO POINT OUT WHO'S TO BLAME FOR YOUR DOWNFALL: THE MEDIA...THE PUBLIC... THE MUSIC BUSINESS... LIBERALISM...THE COURTS... COMMUNISM...CHOLESTEROL... UH...

YOURSELF!!

IGNORE THAT! BILL?.. IGNORE THAT!

ANATOMY OF A SCANDAL, DAY SIX: "THE LONG RIDE BACK HOME..."

YES, YOU REALLY BLEW IT. EMBARRASSED YOURSELF. DASHED YOUR DREAMS. DISAPPOINTED THE WORLD...

AND WORST OF ALL, EVERYONE INVOLVED SUFFERED IN THE END...

..ALMOST EVERYONE.

TAKE ONE EDITH DROCK PEPSI ENDOR.

[95]

ATTENTION! STARTLING ANNOUNCEMENT FOLLOWS:

THE FORMER TUBA PLAYER, CARTOONIST AND BOINGER, **OPUS**, HAS PROCURED A NEW JOB: GARBAGE COLLECTOR.

OPUS? A BLUE-COLLAR WORKINGMAN? HE IS IN TRAINING AS WE SPEAK...

"...THE AFFECTIONS OF PASSING WOMEN CAN BE WON BY THE HOLLERING OF (a) 'HEY, HOT BUNS!', (b) 'YOW! YOW!' OR (c) 'SHAKE IT DON'T BREAK IT, MAMA!' WITH ACCOMPANYING SNORTS..."

MANUAL LABOR MADE EASY

YOU'RE A TRASH MAN?

I BEG YOUR PARDON. I AM A "WASTE-MANAGEMENT ARTISAN."

RIGHT. YOU'RE A GARBAGE MAN.

I'M A WASTE-MANAGEMENT ARTISAN.

YOU EMPTY **TRASH!**

MILO.. DO YOU REMEMBER WHAT THE PRESIDENT CALLED HIS IRANIAN RANSOM SHIPMENTS OF WEAPONS?

"GOODWILL GIFTS."

I'M A "WASTE-MANAGEMENT ARTISAN."

GOOD MORNING, FELLOW WASTE-MANAGEMENT ARTISANS!

WHY THE GLUM FACES? LET'S BE HAPPY IN OUR WORK! COUNT OUR BLESSINGS!...

WHY, JUST KEEP IN MIND HOW THE MANUFACTURING SECTOR OF THE AMERICAN ECONOMY IS STAGNATING WHILE WE IN THE SERVICE INDUSTRIES THRIVE AND PROSPER!

THANK GOD FOR THE **SERVICE** SECTOR!!

SERVICE **THIS**, DUDE.

GOOD MORNING, SIR! I'M YOUR NEW WASTE-MANAGEMENT ARTISAN! ALLOW MYSELF TO INTRODUCE MYSELF BY WAY OF A LITTLE DITTY SUNG TO THE TUNE OF "THE CANDY MAN"...

AHEM!

WHO GETS UP AT SUNRIIISE? SCAMPERS IN THE DEW?...

SNAPS UP ALL THE RUBBISH AND AN APPLE CORE OR TWO?...

THE GARBAGE MAAAN! THE GARBAGE MAN CAN!!

CLICK!

YES?

I WON'T BE PARTY TO THIS, MR. BIGBY.

YOU'VE TOSSED OUT YOUR DREAMS, MR. BIGBY. YOU'VE DISCARDED YOUR HOPES AND THROWN YOUR FAILED AMBITIONS INTO THE RUBBISH CAN OF YOUR YOUTH.

TAKE THEM BACK, MR. BIGBY. RECYCLE THESE OLD AND SPOILED DREAMS.

LORD, HOW THIS JOB IMPROVES ON A METAPHORICAL LEVEL.

PEACH PITS?

MRS. LANGDON, I COULDN'T HELP NOTICING ONE OF YOUR LOVE LETTERS TO MR. LANGDON UNDER THE COFFEE GROUNDS. MAY I READ IT?

"DEAREST WALTER WOOGUMS, WHEN WE KISS, MY TOES ACHE. I LIVE FOR IT. ACHINGLY, ELLIE SUE."

MY NAME'S FRAN.

OF COURSE IT IS.

OH, WALTER WOOGUMS?

YOU PEOPLE SAW THIS COMING A MILE AWAY! WHY DIDN'T YOU STOP ME!?

SOMETIMES I GET TERRIBLY DEPRESSED ABOUT MY NEW JOB...

I THINK OF ALL THOSE OTHER FOLKS OUT THERE STUCK IN POSITIONS OF NO INFLUENCE AND LOWLY STATUS...

I THINK HOW EASY IT WOULD BE TO BECOME A GRUMPY OL' POOP OVER SUCH A SITUATION...

THEN I THINK OF SMILIN' GEORGE BUSH!

STOP THAT.

THE INCREDIBLE STORY BEGAN LAST FRIDAY. BINKLEY WAS IN THE PARLOR GOING INTO SHOCK.

AAAIGH!

WHAT? WHAT?

YEEGBL! GRBLG...

WHAT'S WRONG? THEY FIND JIMMY HOFFA UNDER TAMMY BAKKER'S MAKEUP?

MICHAEL JACKSON FINALLY TURNED INTO GLINDA, THE GOOD WITCH OF THE SOUTH?

NO, NO, NO, NO, NO, NO, NO

NO! NO! NO! NO!

I CERTAINLY HOPE THIS IS CONTINUED.

continued!

IT'S BILL THE CAT, MILO... HE'S... HE'S BEEN **BORN AGAIN!**

BORN AGAIN? BORN AGAIN AS **WHAT?** A DOORKNOB, I HOPE?

NO! HE'S ON TV! HE'S AN EVANGELIST! LOOK! HE'S SHMOOZING FOR DOUGH EVEN AS WE SPEAK!

555-6778

CALLS HIMSELF "FUNDAMENTALLY ORAL BILL."

OH, SOMEBODY PINCH ME.

IT ISN'T A NIGHTMARE! THAT **IS** OUR EX-LEAD BOINGER CALLING HIMSELF "FUNDAMENTALLY ORAL BILL"!

SAYS HE NEEDS FIFTY BUCKS FROM EACH OF US... AND THE SOONER HE GETS IT...

GIVE GIVE GIVE GIVE GIVE GIVE GIVE GIVE

...THE SOONER GOD WILL "CALL HOME" FALWELL, SWAGGART, BAKKER AND ROBERTS.

WIPE OUT THE WHOLE GANG OF FOUR, EH? WHY, NO **TELLING** WHO'LL FALL FOR SUCH A TEMPTING AND SEDUCTIVE PITCH!

FLIP FLIP FLIP FLIP FLIP

MILO! IT'S MY DAD...

HE'S BEEN IN THERE WATCHING FUNDAMENTALLY ORAL BILL ON TV ALL DAY!

ALL DAY!!

HE'S AT THE END OF HIS ROPE, MILO... HE'S VERY VULNERABLE!...

I... I SEE A MAN OUT THERE... HE'S CRYING OUT FOR HELP... HE HAS A LEAKING... A LEAKING... **KIDNEY**...

NO! FUEL PUMP! **FUEL PUMP!!**

SON... LAST NIGHT IN FRONT OF THE TV... I BECAME A BORN-AGAIN FUNDAMENTALIST.

YEAH. NOTICED THE HAIR.

THINGS ARE BECOMING CLEARER... FUNDAMENTAL TRUTHS ARE SUDDENLY REVEALING THEMSELVES AT ANY GIVEN MOMENT!... I... I...

HOLD IT! I FEEL ANOTHER ONE COMING ON... STAND BY!

SON, JIMMY CARTER'S GOING TO HELL FOR GIVING AWAY THE PANAMA CANAL.

YEAH, WELL, DOWN THE HATCH.

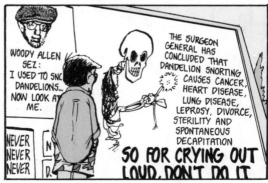

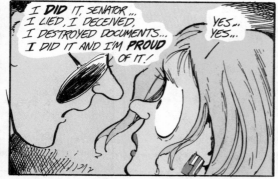

Dear Michael Jackson,

My name is Ronald-Ann. I live on the wrong side of the trax here in Bloom County.

Frankly speaking, all of us in this nayborhood could use a little more money to buy heating oil this winter... also to buy my sister Clara a new doll complete with a head.

Anyway, I red last month that you wanted to spend one millyun dollars to buy The Elephant Man's skeleton...

Well, I, myself would like to offer you a skeleton of an equaly intristing nature. Price: one millyun dollars...

And as soon as I finish this letter, negotiashuns with the donor will begin.

Your Friend,
Ronald-Ann

HOLD IT, BUCKAROOS... WHAT'S THAT YELLOW JUNK ALL OVER HIS LEGS?

YOU DON'T KNOW?

NO, I DO **NOT** KNOW.

MAYBE HIS FATHER NEVER EXPLAINED IT ALL TO HIM...

THEN HE SHOULD'VE LEARNED IT IN HEALTH CLASS...

WHAT? WHAT? **DON'T MESS WITH MY HEAD!**

HE'S GOING TO GET EMBARRASSED.

STEVE...LET ME TELL YOU ALL ABOUT "THE BIRDS AND THE BASSELOPES."

BEFORE THE WARMING RAINS OF SPRING, THE ADULT BASSELOPE WILL FEEL THE INTERNAL STIRRINGS OF NATURE'S FERTILE CALL. FOLLOWING A DEEP AND MYSTERIOUS URGE, THE MATURE MALE WILL SEEK OUT A WILLING AND BOUNTIFUL DANDELION GROVE AND GATHER FRAGRANT POLLEN ABOUT HIS SWOLLEN LEGS AS HE DANCES FEVERISHLY TO THE MUSIC OF WHITNEY HOUSTON. RETURNING TO A FERTILE RHUBARB PATCH, THE MALE WILL SPRINKLE HIS GOLDEN BOOTY ALL OVER THE PLACE AND HOPE AN OFFSPRING OR TWO WILL SPROUT.

"FRAGRANT POLLEN ABOUT HIS SWOLLEN LEGS"?

ESSENTIALLY.

HE'S EMBARRASSED.

WHAT'S GOING ON HERE?!

"SAFE SEX."

WHAT'S THAT, YOU ASK? HOW DID WE RATIONALIZE HOUNDING THAT SINNER OPUS OUT OF TOWN?

WELL, BROTHER PORTNOY AND MYSELF WERE READING SCRIPTURE LAST TUESDAY, AND WE CAME ACROSS "LET HE WHO IS WITHOUT SIN CAST THE FIRST STONE."

RIGHT, BROTHER PORTNOY?

RIGHT. SO WE CAST THAT FIRST MUTHA!

GAZONGAS

OPUS IS GONE. BANISHED... HOUNDED OUT BY A FRIGHTENED FEW. BLOOM COUNTY IS NOW SAFE FROM THE THREAT OF RAMPANT, UNBRIDLED PENGUIN LUST...

THE QUESTION REMAINS: SHOULD ANYONE HAVE DONE MORE TO PREVENT THIS?

QUACK.

RIBBET!

THE QUESTION REMAINS—

MAYBE! JUST POSSIBLY MAYBE!!

HEY.. YOU GUYS ARE MISSING YOUR "ORAL BILL SHOW."

NAW. DON'T WATCH HIM ANYMORE. WE WERE ONCE BORN AGAIN...

BUT NOW WE'RE BORN THRICE.

THREE'S A CHARM!

IT HAPPENED VERY SUDDEN-LIKE...

WE WERE SITTIN' THERE WATCHIN' PHIL DONAHUE AND SUDDENLY—

WHACKO! OPEN-MINDEDNESS!

YOU'VE GOT TO REACH OPUS! TELL HIM EVERYTHING'S BACK TO NORMAL AROUND HERE!!

I FIGURE HE'S REACHED TULSA...

HELLO? TULSA BUS STATION? HAVE YOU SEEN A SHORT FAT GUY WITH A BIG NOSE COME THROUGH? HE WAS PROBABLY EATING OR CRYING...

WHAT?! HE BOUGHT A ONE-WAY TICKET TO OBLIVION?! YOU GOTTA STOP HIM, MAN! QUICK! IS HE STILL THERE?!?

TO BUSES

REMNANTS OF "HERRING McNUGGET" MEAL

DAMP KLEENEX

AS A WEIRD BLOOM COUNTY SUMMER WINDS DOWN, YOUNG LADS WALLOW IN THE BLESSED WATERS OF NORMALCY...

OOF!

LEAP!

..WHILE OTHERS DABBLE IN THE NORMALCY OF A HOBBY... FOR INSTANCE, A NEW HAM RADIO...

PARIS ?... COME IN, PARIS...

Earth Station WBBM 640

HELLO ? MOSCOW ? SANTIAGO ? HEL-LOOOO ?

MEANWHILE, SINISTER ALIEN FORCES GATHER TO WREAK STILL MORE WEIRDNESS UPON THE SCENE...

DENVER ?

ZYGORT DEATH SHIP

CONTINUED!

THIS IS WBBM 640... CINCINNATI ? IS THAT YOU, CINCINNATI ...?

Earth Station WBBM 640

NEGATIVE. THIS IS A ZYGORTHIAN HARVEST SHIP ORBITING 100 MILES ABOVE YOUR TRANSMITTER... ANSWER THE FOLLOWING QUERIES IMMEDIATELY :

ZYGORT DEATH SHIP

ARE EARTHLINGS WHITE OR DARK MEAT ?

Earth Station WBBM 640

CINCINNATI, RACIAL EPITHETS ARE A VIOLATION OF FCC REGULA--

AND IS RED OR WHITE WINE APPROPRIATE FOR THE MEAL ?

Earth Station WBBM 640

YOU MEAN...THIS ISN'T CINCINNATI ?... I'VE MADE ACTUAL CONTACT WITH... ALIEN INTELLIGENCE ?

MORE PRECISELY, WE ARE ZYGORTHIAN RAIDERS FROM THE BLACK NEBULA ...

HEIGHT: 1/2 MILE

ZYGORT DEATH SHIP

SPEAKING FRANKLY, WE'RE HERE TO SLAUGHTER YOUR POPULATION, MAKE HUMAN BEEF JERKY, ENSLAVE YOUR WOMEN AND STARE LURIDLY AT YOUR DAUGHTERS.

ZYGORT DEATH SHIP

E...EXCUSE ME... I'M FLUSH WITH THE HEADY EXHILARATION OF SCIENTIFIC TRIUMPH.

TAKE FIVE.

Earth Station WBBM 640

ALIENS, EH ? DEATH RAYS, EH ? COME TO EAT EARTHLINGS, EH ? SORRY, OLIVER, BUT THIS NEWSMAN REMAINS A CHRONIC SKEPTIC...

LOOK. AN APPETIZER.

SHWAKK!!

HOLD... I SAY HOLD THOSE PRESSES!

SHKKKKKK

WHATCHA WANT, INTERN BLOOM? THINK I GOT A STORY, BOSS.

AN ALIEN RAIDING SHIP HAS BEEN LASER-BLASTING MOST OF TOWN TODAY. THE SVENSON BROTHERS WERE TURNED INTO BACON. MRS. DITBURG WAS SUCKED UP INTO THE SHIP FOR PURPOSES TOO TERRIBLE TO MENTION.

I SUPPOSE YOU EXPECT ME TO BUMP MY JACK KEMP ADULTERY RUMOR STORY TO PAGE TWO!? I DIDN'T SAY THAT!

Bloom Picayune
ZYGORTHIAN RAIDERS ATTACK FROM SPACE
KILL, MAIM, TERRORIZE... WHO ARE THESE MONSTERS? WHAT CAN BE DONE?!

THIS IS ALL ILLEGAL... JUST PLAIN ILLEGAL... YOU WANNA KNOW WHAT NEEDS TO BE DONE?...

SHKKKWAK!!

BY GOSH, A SPECIAL CONGRESSIONAL INVESTIGATING COMMITTEE NEEDS TO GET TO THE BOTTOM OF THIS!! PUGH.

MORE NEWS ON THE ZYGORTHIAN SPACE RAIDERS, DEAR! NOT ONLY HAVE THEY BLASTED OUR CITIES, ENSLAVED OUR WOMEN AND WEAKENED THE DOLLAR...

BUT NOW I READ THEY'VE KIDNAPPED PAT BUCHANAN AND LOCKED HIM IN A ROOM FULL OF AIDS ACTIVISTS. HE'S REPORTEDLY QUITE UPSET.
THEY AIN'T "E.T."

MARK MY WORDS, NOW YER GONNA SEE THE GOVERNMENT GET OUT ITS BIG GUNS AGAINST THIS MENACE!!

WHAT'S THE LETTER, COMMANDER ZORK?! A CONGRESSIONAL SUBPOENA! RETREAT TO PLUTO!!
FEDERAL EXPRESS
ZYGORT DEATH SHIP

BEFORE THE COMMITTEE PROCEEDS TO SANCTIMONIOUSLY DRILL THE LIVING HELL OUT OF THIS WITNESS, I HAVE ONE QUESTION...

ARE WE TO UNDERSTAND THAT YOU ARE THE ALIEN SPACE RAIDER RESPONSIBLE FOR BLASTING OUR CITIES, FRYING OUR CIVILIANS AND SERVING THE ENTIRE MORMON TABERNACLE CHOIR AS HORS D'OEUVRES?

THAT'S CORRECT, EARTHLING SENATOR.
WAG WAG WAG

BIG TROUBLE! HE'S TELEGENIC! DAMMIT, LINDBLUM, YOU SAID HE'D LOOK LIKE "THE BLOB"! NO, I SAID YOU DID!

MR. SPACE INVADER... DO YOU REALIZE THAT THIS CONGRESS PASSED *THE ROLAND AMENDMENT*.. SPECIFICALLY PROHIBITING THE HARVESTING OF GAME-SHOW HOSTESSES AS *ALIEN SLAVE BREEDERS*?

I DID IT. I'M PROUD I DID IT... A DANGEROUS GALAXY DEMANDS DANGEROUS ACTS, SENATOR... I WAS GLAD TO PROVIDE FULL DENIABILITY...

HONOR AND DUTY, SENATOR. THAT IS MY ZYGORTHIAN CODE... I THINK THE PEOPLE OF EARTH CAN APPRECIATE THAT.

ZYGORTHIAN RAIDER

OH, WE DO! WE DO!!

SO WHAT'S A FEW SEX SLAVES?

MY GOD... I BELIEVE HE'S PRESIDENTIAL TIMBER!

NOW, MR. ALIEN MONSTER... ON JULY 23RD, YOU DESTROYED DETROIT, YOU BLEW UP 736 WORKS OF ABSTRACT PUBLIC SCULPTURE ... AND YOU TURNED JOAN COLLINS AND PETER HOLM INTO CABBAGE ... NOW ... ER...

SIR... WHAT *IS* THAT ALL OVER YOUR TABLE?

TELEGRAMS OF SUPPORT.

I QUIT.

RIDLEY, SIT *DOWN*, YOU YELLOW SPUD!

SHOCKED! YES, SHOCKED I AM AT THE TREATMENT OF THIS HEROIC WITNESS...

WELL, THERE HE GOES! SO HE BROKE A FEW RULES... THE GALAXY COULD USE A FEW MORE "TAKE-CHARGE"-TYPE ALIEN MARAUDERS LIKE HIM!

CAUTION SLAVES ON BOARD

BUT I HAVE THIS TERRIBLE VISION OF HIM IN HIS SPACESHIP... SAFELY AWAY FROM GULLIBLE EARTHLING EYES...

...HE STRIPS OFF HIS CHARISMATIC, CUDDLY, "CAN-DO"-KINDA-GUY DISGUISE, REVEALING HIS TRUE, HORRIBLE, BEADY-EYED SHAPE...

WHAT'S HE LOOK LIKE??

ADMIRAL POINDEXTER.

HANG HIM!

GOOD MORNING AND HAPPY BIRTHDAY, DAD.

MY INTERNAL BODY PARTS ARE 40 YEARS OLD.

...47 DELICATE, FRAGILE ORGANS... ALL PUMPING, CRANKING, WHIRRING ALONG WITHOUT A GLITCH FOR 40 YEARS...

MY GOD... MY CAR WON'T RUN FOR TWO MONTHS WITHOUT SOMETHING BUSTING. HOW LONG CAN MY LUCK HOLD OUT??

AW, COME ON, DA—

DON'T JOSTLE THE BED!!

47 FRAGILE ORGANS... 200 MILES OF DELICATE BLOOD VESSELS... 12 MILLION COMPLEX CHEMICAL REACTIONS TO CORRECTLY HAPPEN EVERY SECOND...

EVEN IF I *CAN* KEEP IT ALL FROM BURSTING, BREAKING, SPLITTING, SPURTING OR CORRODING ... I'LL JUST... I'LL...

YOU KNOW.

..GET HIT BY A BUS, FALL ON A DIRTY SOUP SPOON AND CATCH AIDS?

YOU UNDERSTAND.

OKAY. RIGHT. YES. YOU *ARE* 40 YEARS OLD TODAY.

AND YES...THE HUMAN BODY IS UNFATHOMABLY DELICATE IN ITS AWESOME COMPLEXITY... BUT I JUST DON'T SEE WHAT THOSE TWO FACTS HAVE TO DO WITH EACH OTHER.

KLUNK

DON'T LET IT SHAKE YA, POP... *HANG* IN THERE !!

≈SIGH≈

LET'S START YOUR BIRTHDAY OVER AGAIN, DAD.

NOW. LET'S JUST LOOK AT FORTY AS A TIME FOR A *RENEWAL* OF PERSPECTIVE...

LOOK AT THE WORLD AS IF IT'S BRAND-NEW ! SEE THINGS AS IF YOU'VE NEVER SEEN THEM BEFORE !

STARTLING, EH ?

YOU LOOK LIKE BUCKWHEAT.

I..I WANT TO GROW UP... AND BRING DOWN DUMB MEN IN HIGH POSITIONS !

I WANT TO BECOME A GAME-SHOW HOSTESS AND EARN MILLIONS ! I WANT TO STAR IN A JAMES BOND MOVIE ! OR A ROCK VIDEO ! OR BE A PROFESSIONAL CHEERLEADER !

THE OPPORTUNITIES ARE INFINITE !! I MIGHT EVEN BE ... *MISS AMERICA !* YES, I WANT TO GROW UP TO BE ...

...A BIMBO.

YA GOTTA CHASE YER DREAMS, BABY.

JUMPIN' JEHOSHAPHAT! FINALLY, A LETTER FROM OPUS!

OH, GOSH. I DON'T DEAL WITH OVERWHELMING GUILT VERY WELL.

"POSTMASTER: AS MY MOUTH IS DRY FROM TRYING TO SWALLOW THE FACT OF THE RECENT BETRAYAL OF MY FRIENDS, THESE STAMPS WERE MOISTENED WITH TEARS."

HAVING GROWN UP FORCED TO EAT ROTTING SQUID FOR MEALS, PENGUINS MAKE PRACTICED MARTYRS.

DEAR MILO, IT'S ME, YOUR FRIEND OPUS. I AM SAFE AND WORKING.

DRAINED OF ALL SELF-RESPECT, I'M AFRAID THAT I HAVE DRIFTED TO THE UGLIER SIDE OF LIFE'S GRAND STAGE...

NIGHTLY I CHEAPEN AND EXPLOIT MY BODY BEFORE OTHERS MORE MISERABLE THAN ME... A TAWDRY WALTZ OF LOST SOULS. LONELY ARE THE BRAVE, MILO...

MADAM, I *AM* "SHAKING MY BOOTY."

YOU'RE *WADDLING*.

IT'S A NOTE FROM OPUS.

YEAH?! WHAT'S HE DOING?

EXOTIC DANCING FOR A WOMEN-ONLY CLUB IN ARIZONA.

HE'S A *STRIPPER*?

OUR POOR OPUS? DEGRADED ON STAGE? PAMPERING THE TWISTED FANTASIES OF LONELY WOMEN?...

THUMPA THUMPA THUMPA...

SIGH..

YOW!

NEXT: PHIL DONAHUE GETS TO THE BARE FACTS

NOPE. WON'T DO IT. MY CLOTHES STAY ON. AND LADIES... YOU ALL SHOULD BE ASHAMED OF YOURSELVES! GO HOME!

YOUNG MAN... LET ME TELL YOU A STORY...

THERE WAS ONCE A WOMAN... A LONELY WOMAN... WITH A LUMP FOR A HUSBAND, WHO IGNORED HER AND READ "PLAYBOY" AND CHEATED ON HER REGULARLY FOR ALMOST THIRTY YEARS...

AND NOW, AFTER ALL THOSE YEARS, I FIGURE I DESERVE JUST ONE LITTLE NAUGHTY INDULGENCE. DO YOU KNOW WHAT THAT IS, YOUNG MAN?

TO WATCH ME IN MY SKIVVIES?

NO. TO SHOOT HIM.

FINALLY THEY GIVE ME A SCRIPT... WHERE ARE WE? AH. HERE WE GO...

"OPUS IS THUMBING OUTSIDE OF VEGAS. SUDDENLY A CAR DRIVEN BY A CRIMINAL SOCIOPATH SCREECHES UP. OPUS HOPS IN..." SCREECH!

HOWWW-DEE!

THIS... THIS IS WHAT HAPPENS WHEN I MISS ONE STORY CONFERENCE!! YEW KIN SIT NEXT T' ELVIRA HERE...

I'M SO HAPPY. I'M DRIVING TO VEGAS WITH THE BANJO PLAYER FROM "DELIVERANCE" AND HIS PET SLEDGE-HAMMER.

WHAT THIS SCRIPT NEEDS IS A QUICK REWRITE...

ERASE ERASE ERASE... SCRIBBLE SCRIBBLE SCRIBBLE...

NOW WE'RE COOKIN'! ZSA ZSA GABOR CIRCA 1963

GOODBYE! THANKS FOR THE LIFT, ZSA ZSA! SAY HELLO TO EVA FOR ME! VROOOM!

NOW, THIS IS WHAT'S GOING ON: ZSA ZSA HAS DROPPED ME HERE AT CAESAR'S PALACE. NEXT I'LL GO UP TO THE SINATRA SUITE FOR A SCHNOZZ MASSAGE BY JULIE ANDREWS. SEZ IT ALL RIGHT HERE IN THE...ER...

WHERE'S THE SCRIPT? THIS ISN'T VEGAS... WHERE'S THE SCRIPT?

BACK IN THE CAR.

VIRTUALLY SCRIPTLESS, OUR PROTAGONIST WANDERS THE WILDERNESS OF THE AMERICAN LANDSCAPE... GASP... GASP.

NO STORY...NO DIALOGUE... NO ISSUES... NO THEMES... WATER...

HE'S COMPLETELY WITHOUT DIRECTION... AUGH..

HE IS NOT, HOWEVER, WITHOUT HIS NEEDLE-SHARP INSTINCTS FOR A SNAPPY METAPHOR... BOY! I FEEL LIKE THE DEMOCRATIC PARTY!

I HAVE A NICE COLD GLASS OF CHOCOLATE "BOSCO"... JUST HOW YOU USED TO LIKE IT, DEAR.

QUICK! LEMME HAVE IT, MA!

FIRST TELL YOUR MOTHER THAT YOU MISS HER.

I MISS YA, MA!

TELL HER THAT YOU LOVE HER!

I LOVE YA, MA! I LOVE YA!

TELL HER WHY YOU HAVEN'T MARRIED A NICE CATHOLIC GIRL AND HAD TEN KIDS BY YOUR AGE.

I LOVE YA, MA!

OPUS, DEAR... I MAY ONLY BE A HEAT HALLUCI-NATION, BUT I'M **STILL** YOUR MOTHER AND YOU'LL LISTEN TO ME...

NOW GET YOUR WITS ABOUT YOU AND JUST GET YOUR LITTLE FANNY OUT OF THIS DESERT MESS!

I DIDN'T RAISE MY SON TO BE A QUITTER, DID I?

NO, MA.

AND YOU WILL TAKE CARE OF THAT BIG ZIT ON YOUR NOSE, WON'T YOU, DEAR?

THAT **IS** MY NOSE, MA.

I'M SAVED!! AN OUTPOST OF AMERICAN CIVILIZATION!!

7eleven

GONZO GULP 79¢

OH HAPPY DAY! SERVE UP ONE "JUMBO GONZO GULP" OF DIET PEPSI, MISTER CLERK!!

HE DOESN'T SPEAK ENGLISH.

IT'S OPUS! HE'S FORGIVEN US! HE'S COMING HOME!!

WHAT? DID WE MISS YOU? WHY, WE'VE BEEN COUNTING THE HOURS TILL YOUR RETURN! RIGHT!

YOUR ROOM? UH...WHY, WE HAVEN'T TOUCHED A THING, OF COURSE ... RIGHT... A VIRTUALLY SACRED MEMORIAL TO YOUR ANTICI-PATED RETURN...

OUT? I JUST SIGNED A LEASE!

SO WE'RE GOING CONDO. VAMOOSE!

LET'S JUST GET TO THE FACTS: DURING TEATIME ON A RECENT BLUSTERY SUNDAY, A STRONG GUST CAUGHT A LOCAL BASSELOPE'S EARS, AND HE DID, IN FACT, BECOME AIRBORNE.

SAILING EAST, HE FOUND MRS. NUSBAUM'S LAUNDRY LINE, AND IN PARTICULAR, SHORTS BELONGING TO MR. NUSBAUM, WHO LATER BLAMED THEIR DISAPPEARANCE ON SOCIALISTS.

SHUUMP!

AT 4:16 P.M., A NEAR MISS WITH A UFO WAS REPORTED BY DELTA AIRLINES, WHICH WAS HAVING A BAD YEAR ANYWAY.

5:01 P.M. PINKERTON AIR FORCE BASE FIRED A GROUND-TO-AIR HEAT-SEEKING MISSILE AT A SUSPECTED IRANIAN SUICIDE PARATROOPER WEARING BOXER SHORTS. IT MISSED.

ZING!

SHKKKK!!

GLAM!

BY 6 P.M., THE MEADOW CRISIS TEAM HAD MOBILIZED AND DID EVENTUALLY BRING THE SITUATION UNDER CONTROL. WITH SOME DIFFICULTY.

THE FAA PROMISED A FULL INVESTIGATION. NEVERTHELESS, THERE WAS SOME IRRESPONSIBLE AND PREMATURE SPECULATION REGARDING THE EXACT CAUSE OF THE AFTERNOON'S UNFORTUNATE EVENTS.

FORGET TO SAY OUR PRAYERS, DID WE?

I SAY... YOU ARE A Wild Animal, AREN'T YOU?

YEP.

EXCUSE ME, BUT HAVE YOU EVER BEEN TRAPPED, SHOT, POISONED, PIERCED, NETTED, CLUBBED, HOOKED, PICKLED, BLUDGEONED, BEATEN, BATTERED OR BEHEADED?

NOPE.

EVER BEEN SKINNED, SMOKED, STUFFED, GUTTED, FRIED, FILETED, BASTED, BROILED, BARBECUED, ROASTED OR TOASTED?

NOPE.

... CAUGHT, CAGED, TESTED, DISPLAYED, TRAINED, REINED, MAIMED, INJECTED, INFECTED, REJECTED, TORMENTED OR TORTURED?

NOPE.

YOU JUST RUN AROUND ALL DAY DOIN' NOTHIN'?

YEP.

HERE'S ONE!

BLAM!

SWISH!

PHOOM!

BLAM!

BLAM

WOOOSH!!

BLAM!!

SNAP!

YOU'RE HOME.

I AM HOME.

I'M SO SORRY. IT MUST HAVE BEEN AWFUL OUT THERE...

WELL, IT WAS NO STROLL IN A BED OF ROSES.

...WANDERING... MEANDERING... LOST IN A CREATIVE WILDERNESS WITHOUT PURPOSE, DIRECTION... OR EVEN A SCRIPT.

SOUNDS LIKE A MADONNA MOVIE.

RIGHT! GOOD! EVEN BETTER THAN THE DEMOCRAT METAPHOR!

UH... ON BEHALF OF THE BORN-AGAIN MEMBERS OF MEADOW SOCIETY, I'D LIKE YOU TO KNOW THAT DESPITE OUR EARLIER BEHAVIOR, TO US YOU'LL ALWAYS BE... UH...

..OUR PENGUIN-LUSTING INFIDEL WHO'S GONNA BURN BURN BURN!!

WHACK!!

..OUR GOOD FRIEND.

THANKS.

UH.. MILO HAD US ALL GET YOU A WELCOME-BACK GIFT. HERE.

A "PLAYBOY"? I THOUGHT YOU WERE BORN AGAIN, TOO.

I AM. I'M A RIGHTEOUS, GOD-FEARING DUDE.

UH-HUH.

WHY YA LOOKIN' AT ME LIKE THAT?

HEY, IT'S COOL... THAT'S JESSICA HAHN!

OH OH OH.

I'M AMAZED...

"JESSICA HAHN NUDE.." "POLICEWOMEN UNDRESSED..." "THE GIRLS OF NASA"..

WHAT COULD POSSIBLY CONVINCE AN OTHERWISE RATIONAL WOMAN TO DISPLAY HER PRIVATES TO THE MILLIONS OF PIMPLY-FACED COLLEGE BOYS WHO READ THIS STUFF?

"HEF" AIMING A FLAME-THROWER AT HER PARENTS' HEADS?

NO, I UNDERSTAND FREE WILL IS INVOLVED.

[121]

SAY... ANXIETIES... WHAT'RE Y'ALL DOING OVER THERE COWERING IN THE CORNER ?
YEEK!
SHSHH!
WHATSA MATTER ? SOMEBODY ELSE IN THE CLOSET ? WHY... IT'S TAMMY FAYE !! WHAT'S GOING ON, TAMMY ?
I THOUGHT I'D SING...
NO SINGING!!

SO! TAMMY BAKKER IS IN MY ANXIETY CLOSET AND EVERYONE'S HAVING A COW ABOUT IT, EH ?
WELL, IT'S A CHEAP SHOT! JIM AND TAMMY HAVE HAD A ROUGH TIME! THEY DESERVE MORE RESPECT THAN THIS! SHAME ON YOU!
LOOK WHAT YOU'VE DONE... TAMMY'S STARTING TO CRY...
NO CRYING!!
FOOOSH!!

POINK! POINK!
AAIGH!
IT'S ONLY ME, YOUR OFFSPRING'S MOST PROMINENT ANXIETY...
WE THOUGHT YOU SHOULD KNOW THAT TAMMY BAKKER IS IN BINKLEY'S CLOSET CRYING, AND WE'RE HAVING SOME FLOODING PROBLEMS. THANK YOU.
I'M GOING TO FILE THIS UNDER "BED-WETTING" AND FORGET THAT MY BOY IS A
LOON!!

HI, STEVE. YOUR MOTHER CAME BY.
WHAT?! YA TOLD HER I WAS OUT OF TOWN, I HOPE!
STEVE, REMEMBER WHEN I WAS USING THE REST ROOM IN THE DRUGSTORE DOWNTOWN ?
YEAH.
REMEMBER HOW YOU TOLD THE LADIES' SEWING CLUB IT WAS OKAY TO GO IN ?
YEAH. SO ?
SO, I LET YOUR MOTHER INTO YOUR ROOM AND TOLD HER THAT YOU'RE SMOKING AGAIN.
GO AHEAD. SLIT MY WRISTS.

MOM! I TOLD YOU TO **CALL** BEFORE FLYING OUT!! SMELLS LIKE A TURKISH BATH IN HERE.

WHAT'S UP? YOU DIVORCING EDGAR? I ACCIDENTALLY FOUND SOME COCAINE BETWEEN THE BOARDS UNDER YOUR DRESSER, BUT I THINK IT'S JUST ROACH DROPPINGS.

STOP SCATTERING BIBLES AROUND THE PLACE, MA. BELL-BOTTOMS! WHO ARE YOU? SAMMY DAVIS, JR.?

HI, MA. OH, STEVIE, WE SHOULD TALK LIKE THIS MORE OFTEN!

YOU'RE THIRTY, STEVIE! YOU SHOULD HAVE A WIFE! YOU'RE GOING TO END UP LIKE POOR LIBERACE... DYING LONELY WITHOUT EVER HAVING MET THE RIGHT WOMAN!

EXCUSE ME, MA, BUT I DON'T THINK LIBERACE'S MAIN FOCUS WAS EXACTLY **WOMEN!**

WUMP!

STEVIE... WHA--WHAT EXACTLY DO YOU MEAN? NOTHIN', MA. I JUST MEANT THAT HE MUST NEVER HAVE MET YOU...

STEVIE... YOU'RE SAYING THAT LIBERACE "WALKED ON THE OTHER SIDE OF THE FENCE"? SO TO SPEAK, MA.

AND MANY OF MY OTHER ROMANTIC MUSICAL HEROES "GO UP THE DOWN STAIRCASE"? IN SO MANY WORDS.

EVEN **HE** "PUTTS FROM THE ROUGH"? HOLE IN ONE, MA.

I'LL MISS HIM. HE KNEW THE VALUE OF A BILLION. I WROTE A RHYME ABOUT HIM SOME YEARS AGO...

OPUS THE RHYMING BARD

"THE WIND DOTH TASTE SO BITTERSWEET, LIKE JASPER WINE AND SUGAR, I BET IT'S BLOWN THRU OTHERS' FEET..."

"...LIKE THOSE OF CASPAR WEINBERGER."

I WONDER IF WE'LL MAKE IT WITHOUT HIM... "CARLUCCI. CAR SMOOCHY. CARP SUSHI..." I'M NOT OPTIMISTIC.

SOON FAMILY MEMBERS WILL BEGIN ARRIVING IN BIG DOMESTICALLY PRODUCED CARS...

DOGS WILL CURL UP BEFORE FIRES... WOMEN WILL COLLECT IN THE KITCHEN AND ROAST ANIMALS... MEN WILL DRINK EGGNOG AND DISCUSS MANLY THINGS...

AND THEN EVERYONE WILL GO TO CHURCH AND PARTICIPATE IN A WESTERN RELIGION OF THEIR CHOICE! BOY!

CHRISTMAS IS SO REPUBLICAN.

MAYBE BINKLEY'S RIGHT. CHRISTMAS IS KIND OF REPUBLICAN.

UNCLE FRED WILL RUB LITTLE BOBBY'S HEAD. DAD WILL STOKE THE WARM FIRE... MOM WILL BRING OUT THE TURKEY —· DAD'LL CARVE, OF COURSE. ULTRA-NORMAN ROCKWELL.

A TIME TO CELEBRATE THE NUCLEAR FAMILY! VERY REPUBLICAN.

HAVE A FAMILY?

A MOM. SHE GAVE ME AWAY WHEN I WAS TWO. VERY LIBERTARIAN.

HERE. IT'S A McDONALD'S GIFT CERTIFICATE FOR A "BIG MAC" MERRY CHRISTMAS.

OH, THANK YOU!

AND THIS IS FOR YOU... A MINIATURE BRONZE BUST OF MYSELF THAT I PAINSTAKINGLY CRAFTED AS A GESTURE OF OUR ETERNAL FRIENDSHIP.

YESSIR.. SIXTEEN LONG MONTHS IT TOOK...

HERE'S ANOTHER ONE FOR A LARGE FRIES!

NO, NO... WOULDN'T THINK OF IT...

OH, PORTNOY!

OH, NO... oo..

GET AWAY FROM ME, OPUS! YOU JUST WANNA GIVE ME ONE OF YOUR ABSURDLY SPECTACULAR CHRISTMAS GIFTS, SO YOU CAN ACT SMUG ABOUT IT ALL YEAR LONG!!

I HAVE SOMETHING FOR YOU...

NO! GET AWAY!!

HERE. IT'S A SWEATER I KNITTED OUT OF TEN YEARS' WORTH OF MY BELLY-BUTTON LINT.

THANKS. HERE'S YOUR YELLOWSTONE SOUVENIR ASHTRAY.

MERRY CHRISTMAS, MILO.

OH, NO, YOU DON'T...

EVERY CHRISTMAS YOU FEEL DEPRESSED ABOUT YOUR MOM, AND EVERY CHRISTMAS YOU DEAL WITH IT BY PLAYING **THE MARTYR** WITH YOUR AWE-INSPIRING, UNMATCHABLE GIFTS! WELL, I WON'T BE PART OF YOUR GUILT TRIP!!

HEY... C'MON... DON'T DO THAT... LOOK, I'M SORRY. I'D LOVE TO RECEIVE YOUR GIFT...

SNIFF!

AH. THE ENTIRE GREAT WALL OF CHINA PERSONALLY CARVED TO 1/1000 SCALE IN SOLID BRASS.

GOLD. MELTED DOWN MY FILLINGS.

WELL, BINKLEY, I BOUGHT THE EXCLUSIVE COLLECTION OF MICHAEL JACKSON'S POST-SURGICAL NOSE AND FACIAL BONE FRAGMENTS FOR YOUR CHRISTMAS PRESENT...

REALLY?!

THEN I REALIZED SUCH A GRAND GESTURE MIGHT PUT YOU IN AN AWKWARD POSITION...

HEY! NOT TO WORRY!

...SO I GOT YOU A CALENDAR INSTEAD.

OH.

YEP. THIS IS RIGHT.

"BUNS"?

"AND THUS THE BABY JESUS WAS BORN UNTO THIS WORLD..."

"AND PEOPLE REJOICED AND SAID, 'FOR ALL TIME TO COME, LET THIS DAY BE A DAY FOR UNDERSTANDING, LOVE...

"...AND PEACE AMONG ALL MEN.'"

WHERE'S BOBBY?

CLICK!

RAMBO

STEVE DALLAS FINE ATTORNEY

MR. DALLAS... I NEED A LAWYER.

MY BROTHER BOBBY HAS BECOME A HOMICIDAL "RAMBO"-PHILE... HE GOT ENOUGH WAR TOYS FOR CHRISTMAS TO FILL A U.S. ARMS SHIPMENT TO IRAN. I THINK WE SHOULD SUE.

SUE WHO?

I UNDERSTAND "THE TOP" IS A GOOD PLACE TO START...

CLAUS TOYS

#1 NORTH POLE

COURT DOCUMENT SUBPOENA

STEVIE! GLENDA WAZINCHINSKI JUST TOLD ME YOU'RE SUING *SANTA CLAUS*!! WELL!!

MY SON, THE SANTA ATTACKER! I'M SO PROUD! WHO ELSE ARE YOU GUNNING FOR? MOTHER TERESA? SHIRLEY TEMPLE?!

LOOK, MA... I WORK FOR MY CLIENT. IF SHE SAYS SUE SANTA CLAUS, I SUE SANTA CLAUS! YOU *KNOW* HOW THIS WORKS, MA.

NOW C'MON... (*KISS* *KISS*) WHAT'S FOR DINNER?

BAMBI.

DISCUSSION CLOSED, MA. I'VE BEEN HIRED TO SUE SANTA CLAUS FOR MAKING WAR TOYS, AND THAT'S *THAT*.

..AND *DON'T*, AS USUAL, TRY TO TAKE REVENGE FOR MY DEFIANCE BY GOING AFTER MY VULNERABLE SPOTS... THE ONES YOU KNOW SO *DARNED* WELL.

ME?

YEAH, YOU.

WAIT! FREEZE!

WHAT? WHAT?!

YOUR HAIRLINE MOVED.

TODAY WE DRAG SANTA CLAUS TO COURT, MR. DALLAS. IT'S FRIGHTENING!

IT COULD GET UGLY, MONICA.

..NO DOUBT HE'LL BE SENDING OUT HIS HIGH-CALIBER, PIN-STRIPED LEGAL GUNS...

A MOMENT, PLEASE, COUNSELOR.

PLEASE ADVISE YOUR CLIENT THAT UNLESS SHE HALTS HER SPURIOUS SUIT AGAINST *MY* CLIENT, HE'LL HAVE LITTLE RECOURSE BUT TO LEAVE DEAD SPIDERS IN HER STOCKING NEXT YEAR.

TAKIN' OFF THE GLOVES, EH? NO DEAL! NO DEAL!!

NOW, BOBBY, YOUR SISTER SAYS YOU RECEIVED 37 TOYS OF DEATH AND HUMAN DESTRUCTION FOR CHRISTMAS, CORRECT?

THINK THAT'S AN APPROPRIATE WAY TO CELEBRATE JESUS' BIRTHDAY?

TURNING INTO A LITTLE WAR-GLORIFYING SOCIOPATH, AREN'T WE, BOBBY?

— BOBBY?

.YOUR WITNESS.

LAWYERS DIE.

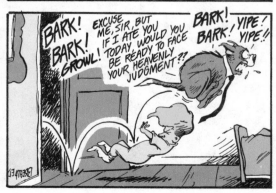

SO! DID YA WIN THE BIG COURT CASE? FOR ONCE?

SHUT UP OR I'LL STUFF LEECHES UP YOUR NOSE.

O FOR 92, IS IT?

GRRRRR...

DO YOU REALIZE THEY'VE GOT PHOTO SATELLITES UP THERE THAT CAN SEE THE COLOR OF OUR EYES...

NO DOUBT A DISTURBING REVELATION TO ALL THOSE CLANDESTINE CRIME COMMITTERS.

... NOT TO MENTION US SURREPTITIOUS NOSE PICKERS.

OLIVER TOLD ME, THEY HAVE SATELLITES THAT CAN SEE US. ANYTIME. DOING THINGS IN PRIVATE.

WHAT THINGS?

PRIVATE THINGS! YOU KNOW!

LIKE WHAT?

OH, YOU KNOW... THOSE UGLY LITTLE MINOR THINGS WE ALL DO... BUT NOT IN FRONT OF EACH OTHER... GROSS THINGS WE NEVER IMAGINE CHRISTIE BRINKLEY DOING BUT THAT SHE PROBABLY DOES...

OH, YOU KNOW...

I'M TO UNDERSTAND YOU DO THESE THINGS?

THEY'RE WATCHING FROM ABOVE!! PRIVACY IS HISTORY! DOES ANYBODY CARE? WHERE WILL IT LEAD?! HELLO?

SIGH...

SCRATCH SCRATCH

USA TODAY

GOV'T. PHOTO SHOWING UGLY MAN SCRATCHING PITS

I RAIDED THE BOOKSTORE FOR SELF-HELP BOOKS TO HELP ME COPE WITH MY MIDLIFE SNIT...

AREN'T THEY WONDERFUL? A VERITABLE TOWER OF PSYCHOBABBLE!

MY GOODNESS, IT'S GREAT TO LIVE IN AN AGE WHERE THE EMOTIONALLY DISCOMBOBULATED CAN SO EXPERTLY TREAT THEMSELVES!

WHAT, OH WHAT, MUST OUR ANCESTORS HAVE DONE?!

TAKEN A HOT BATH.

THANK GOODNESS FOR ALL THE PSYCHOBABBLE SELF-HELP AVAILABLE... THESE CERTAINLY ARE TOUGH TIMES FOR PEOPLE TO COPE WITH...

RIGHT. HOW EASY THEY MUST HAVE HAD IT IN THE OLD DAYS...

CIVIL WARS! PESTILENCE! PLAGUE! MASSIVE STARVATION! SLAVERY! INDIAN ATTACKS! MAN-EATING BEARS! EMOTIONALLY, MUST'VE BEEN A PICNIC!!

HEY! THEY MOVED "COSBY" TO TUESDAYS AT EIGHT! I WAS WOBBLY FOR A WEEK!!

THE MIGHTY HUMANISTIC, RATIONALISTIC, ATHEISTIC SCIENTIST PREPARES TO GIVE HIMSELF OVER TO AN ANNUAL SPRINGTIME MOMENT OF WILD ABANDON...

THE UNIVERSE IS A LITTLE TOO DARNED ORDERLY TO BE JUST A BIG ACCIDENT!!

MY MOUTH FEELS UNCOMFORTABLY DRY.

CAN YOU BREATHE?

YEAH. BUT MY TONGUE IS KINDA STICKY-FEELING... YUCKY... SORTA STARCHY.. YA KNOW?

THAT'S IT? ARE YOU CHOKING?

NO. MY TONGUE IS STARCHY.

DON'T CALL AGAIN! LET'S HOPE YOU'VE LEARNED A LESSON!

CLICK!

THE LESSON BEING, I SUPPOSE, NOT TO DIAL 911 JUST FOR HAVING EATEN AN UNDERRIPE BANANA.

HELLO? 911? YES! HOW CAN WE HELP?!

THERE'S A 465-POUND WOMAN ACROSS THE STREET PRUNING HER AZALEAS WEARING A PAIR OF PEA-SOUP-GREEN HOT PANTS!! WHAT'S THE EMERGENCY?

FROM A TASTE PERSPECTIVE, IT'S A CRISIS OF BIBLICAL PROPORTIONS.

OUCH! OUCH! HELLO? 911 EMERGENCY HOTLINE? I KNOW THAT VOICE!.. OUCH YEEK

...SO WHAT'S THE EMERGENCY? YOUR HAMBURGER MEAT TOO FATTY? NO! I HAVE A REAL MEDICAL CRISIS!

BREAK YOUR NECK? SUMMER'S COMING UP... I WAXED MY LEGS.

SO? RIPPED MY KNEECAPS OFF. THEY'RE BEHIND THE TOILET. OOCH.. YEEK...

WHO'S THERE? YOUR WORST ANXIETY, BUDDY BOY! PROGRESSIVE WOMEN!

WOMEN WHO'LL OPEN DOORS FOR YOU! ..WHO'LL CHOOSE THE WINE AT DINNER! WOMEN WHO'LL TAKE YOUR HAND AND LEAD YOU THROUGH A CROWD!

FINE WITH ME. FINE WI--? SAY, AREN'T YOU S. DALLAS?

M. BINKLEY. WRONG CLOSET, GIRLS!

ACTUALLY, MADAM, I'M QUITE THE PROGRESSIVE ON WOMEN'S ISSUES. YOU'RE LOOKING FOR STEVE'S CLOSET. COULD YOU TELL US THE WAY?

SURE. GO WEST PAST THE FURNACE... TURN RIGHT, THEN A LEFT...ANOTHER LEFT...PAST THE SNORKLEWACKER, THEN RIGHT TO EAST. GOT IT? NO.

BOY, DON'T GALS HAVE THE WORST TIME WITH DIRECTIONS?

BACK HERE, GIRLS!!

THE WHOLE UGLY AFFAIR BEGAN THE WAY THESE THINGS ALWAYS DO — WITH OPUS IN THE VICINITY...

STEVE? YEAH.

DO YOU BELIEVE SPACE ALIENS EVER KIDNAP PEOPLE WITH POWERFUL TRACTOR BEAMS?

WHY?

RRRRRRRRRr!!

HEY! HEY!!

MOOT QUESTION!!

STEVE'S BEEN NABBED BY ALIENS!

SWOOOPED UP INTO THE JAWS OF ALIEN DEATH! IT WAS HORRIBLE!!

WE'VE GOT TO NOTIFY THE AUTHORITIES!

OPUS IS DOING THAT RIGHT NOW!!

HELLO?! 911?!

CLICK!

THE BLOOM PICAYUNE

LOCAL LAWYER KIDNAPPED BY SPACE ALIENS!

by Staff Reporter MILO BLOOM

EYEWITNESS

"YESTERDAY, STEVE DALLAS WAS VIOLENTLY ABDUCTED BY A PASSING ALIEN SPACESHIP...

PUSH

CITY DESK

"...THE ONLY WITNESS WAS LEFT A CONFUSED, BLABBERING, FISH ENTRAILS-EATING MANIAC...

PUSH

"LATER IT WAS DETERMINED HE WAS JUST BEING HIMSELF."

WELL, EXCUSE THE HECK OUT OF ME.

PUSH

CITY DESK

STOLEN FROM THE WARM EMBRACE OF TERRA FIRMA...

...THE STOLEN EARTH ATTORNEY ORBITS SOMEWHERE ABOVE IN THE EVIL HANDS OF SCHEMING ALIENS...

...BUT WHATEVER THEIR NEFARIOUS PLANS, STEVE WILL HAVE THE FORMIDABLE POWER OF HUMAN INSTINCT TO BETTER FACE THEM!

ZYGOR'S KIDNAP SPECIAL X-17

ZOLTAR! FETCH ELVIS'S BRAIN!

DO YOU UNDERSTAND THE WORD "LAWSUIT"?! DO YOU UNDERSTAND THE WORDS "PUNITIVE DAMAGES"?!

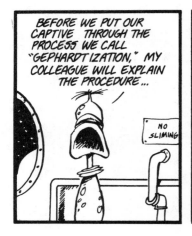

BY NOW, STEVE HAD BEEN MISSING FOR SEVERAL WEEKS. THE PESSIMIST'S (OR OPTIMIST'S) VIEW WAS THAT, SADLY, HE HAD "GONE TO BE WITH THE LORD," AS OPUS WOULD SAY.

'NOTHER WORDS, "DEAD AS A DOORKNOB."

BY AND BY, A WAKE WAS CALLED IN STEVE'S MEMORY. FRIENDS GATHERED TO REMEMBER...

STEVE WAS A GOOD MAN...

HE WAS AN HONEST MAN... A DECENT MAN... A SINCERE MAN...

ONLY ROOT BEER

HE WAS A ASUEBODY.

BUT HE WAS A SINCERE ANOBODY !!

I... HAVE BEEN ASSSKED... TO SAY A FEW WORDTH ABOUT THE FINER QUALITIES OF OUR GOOD, DECEASED FRIEND STEVE DALLAS... AHEM.

NOT JUST ROOT BEER

SNORT

URP

HE COULD SPIT FORTY FEET.

FOR WHICH WE LOVED HIM LIKE A BROTHER. GOOD NIGHT.

STEVE DALLAS HAD PASSED ON WITHOUT A WILL. A MEMBER OF HIS WAKE WAS THUS DISPATCHED TO FETCH HIS EARTHLY BOOTY.

STEVE'S STUFF

IT INCLUDED: LAW BOOKS, A FRAT PIN, LOOSE CHANGE AND A BOTTLE OF "OLD SPICE," WHICH PORTNOY ACCIDENTALLY DRANK, CAUSING HIM TO RUN AROUND THINKING HE WAS "AUNT BEA."

ANDY? OPIE?

A BOX OF "TROJANS" WAS ALSO FOUND AND, AFTER MUCH DEBATE, FINALLY IDENTIFIED AS POSSIBLY BEING MICROWAVE JELL-O MOLDS.

HMM.

BUT HE HATED COOKING!

STEVE'S STUFF

THE LATTER WERE FILLED WITH WATER AND DELIVERED AIRBORNE UNTO MRS. PAULA PEGWHISTLE'S PASSING PONTIAC... WHICH PRETTY WELL WRAPPED THINGS THE HECK UP FOR THE NIGHT.

BLAM!

STEVIE, STEVIE! STEVIE, STEVIE! ...WE HARDLY KNEW YE!

SNIFF!

SAY... WHAT'S THAT UP THERE? AN ALIEN SPACECRAFT?!

SSHHKKK!

≳GULP!≲ S-STEVE?

JEEPERS! WHAT HAPPENED?

-- TO BE CONTINUED! OR MAYBE IT WON'T! YA NEVER KNOW, DO YA?

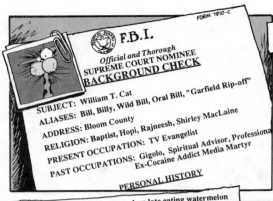

GIMME THE BAD NEWS...

THIS YEAR YOU OWE THE AMERICAN MILITARY-INDUSTRIAL COMPLEX #23,937.42

AAIGH!!

YA KNOW, MILO, IN FLORIDA THEY LIKE TO EAT THE CLAWS OF A CERTAIN SPECIES OF CRAB... THE STONE CRAB...

EACH YEAR THEY CATCH MILLIONS OF STONE CRABS, RIP OFF JUST ONE OF THEIR CLAWS AND THEN TOSS THEM BACK IN...

BLEEDING AND MUTILATED, THE LITTLE CRABS STRUGGLE TO SURVIVE AND GROW BACK THEIR STOLEN CLAW... ONLY TO GET CAUGHT AND HAVE IT YANKED OFF AGAIN NEXT YEAR!!

IF YOU HAVEN'T GUESSED BY NOW, I'M FEELING A LITTLE LIKE A STONE CRAB MYSELF!! GOOD DAY!

NEXT.

THANKS.

JEEZ... COULD THIS JOB POSSIBLY GET ANY MORE DEPRESSING?

GIMME THE BAD NEWS.

SEE THAT BLINKING STAR? THE LIGHT WE'RE SEEING FROM IT IS 537 MILLION YEARS OLD.

IMAGINE!

WHILE MY ANCESTORS CRAWLED FROM THE PRIMORDIAL SOUP, THIS STARLIGHT WAS ALREADY HURTLING TOWARD EARTH...

ON IT CAME... WHILE THE DINOSAURS RULED... AND THE PHARAOHS BUILT THEIR PYRAMIDS... AND ROME BURNED... AND THE EARTH TREMBLED IN WORLD WARS... AND BUSH ACCUSED DOLE OF CRONYISM...

...DOWN CAME THE LITTLE STAR'S SHIMMERING LIGHT! DOWN TO FINALLY FALL UPON MY FACE!

RIGHT HERE! RIGHT NOW! LO! I AM THE CENTER OF THE UNIVERSE! I AM ONE WITH THE MILLENNIA!

HOLD IT. IT'S JUST A FIREFLY.

THE MILLENNIA MAN IS OFF TO THE BATHTUB.

A BAT JUST ATE IT.

STEVE'S NOT HERE, QUICHE. HE'S IN COURT TODAY. YEAH, I DON'T LIKE TO THINK ABOUT IT, EITHER...

...HE MURDERED THE ENTIRE MOOSE LODGE... STABBED THEM. BRUTALLY. WITH THEIR OWN ANTLERS.

THE DEFENDANT IS A LOATHSOME, PIG-FACED, VICIOUS ANIMAL WHO SHOULD BE CHAINED IN A VERY SMELLY SEWER!!

HE'S ALSO YOUR CLIENT, COUNSELOR.

WHAT AM I SUPPOSED TO DO? FIB?

YEAH! YEAH!

95 YEARS AT HARD LABOR! I DON'T UNNERSTAN... YA TOLD DA JURY I WAS A PIG-FACED, SEWER-SCUM RAT.

DID I LIE, REGINALD?

WELL... NO.

DID YOU KILL THOSE 97 MOOSE-LODGE MEMBERS WITH THEIR OWN ANTLERS?

I DON'T LIKE MOOSE.

SO WHAT KIND OF CITIZEN WOULD I BE IF I LIED TO GET OBVIOUS PSYCHO-PATHS BACK ON THE STREET?

YOU'DN BE A LAWYER.

I'LL VISIT YOUR MOTHER, REGINALD.

HI, MA.

SWEET BABY JESUS!

YOU REMEMBERED A LONELY MOTHER'S BIRTHDAY?

MADE YOU A CARD, TOO. I DREW YOU AND ME HOLDING HANDS.

STEVEN MILHOUSE DALLAS... YOU GET YOUR BRAIN ZAPPED BY ALIENS OR SOMETHING?

I'LL COOK UP A HAM, MA.

FIRE BACK®

"WHERE THE READERS RESPOND"

TODAY: MR. CHARLES RAYMOND FOXWORTH... PRESIDENT OF THE AMERICAN ASSOC. FOR THE ADVANCEMENT OF PEOPLE WITH FACIAL HAIR.

LAST WEEK, THIS FEATURE DISPLAYED A BEARDED PERSON CHARAC-TERIZED AS A VIOLENT LUNATIC. THIS IS PURE, IRRESPONSIBLE BIGOTRY.

PEOPLE WITH FACIAL HAIR ARE OFTEN DOCTORS, JUDGES, BAGGAGE HANDLERS AND OTHER LAW-ABIDING CITIZENS. WE STRONGLY RESENT THE STEREOTYPE SUGGESTING OTHERWISE.

"FIRE BACK®" WELCOMES OPPOSING VIEWPOINTS. WRITE ℅ THIS NEWSPAPER.

...IN FACT, THIS SORT OF THING MAKES ME SO MAD I COULD STRANGLE A MANATEE IN THE NUDE... " AARGH..

THE CHAIR ACKNOWLEDGES THAT A NOMINATION VOTE IS NOT BINDING UNLESS THE V.P. NOMINEE IS IN ATTENDANCE...

SO ONCE AGAIN... ALL IN FAVOR OF OPUS AS OUR '88 V.P. NOMINEE?...

AYE!!

WHEW! DOES PARTICIPATORY DEMOCRACY PUT A LUMP IN YOUR THROAT, TOO?

MMPH.

YOU! YOU RAILROADED ME INTO BEING NOMINATED SECOND BANANA TO A FRUIT-CAKE!!

"BILL THE CAT" IS HIS NOM DE PLUME.

YES, WELL, AT THE MOMENT, HE'S PLUME PASSED OUT AGAIN.

IF SAM DONALDSON SHOULD ASK, HE'S JUST IN A RELIGIOUS FERVOR.

ACK SNORT THPPT!

WHAT'S THAT? SPEAKING IN TONGUES?

GONNA BE A LONG CAMPAIGN.

REPRESENTATIVES FROM THE A.A.P.O.P.T.A.P. ARE HERE TO MEET WITH BILL.

HE'S PASSED OUT IN THE DEN.

MIGHT THEY SETTLE FOR A LOWLY V.P.?

WHY NOT?

SO WHO ARE THEY?

THE AMERICAN ASSOC. OF P.O.'D PTA PARENTS.

YO! WAKE UP THERE!! UP AND AT 'EM!

WAK! WAK! WAK! WAK!

CONGRATULATIONS ON YOUR V.P. NOMINATION, OPUS...

CRUNCH CRUNCH

DRIED HERRING PITUITARY GLANDS

BY THE WAY, I'D LIKE YOU TO SAY A FEW WORDS AT A SPECIAL FUND-RAISING CONCERT I'M ORGANIZING TO BENEFIT A TROUBLED INDUSTRY...

MUNCH MUNCH

..A WHOLE AMERICAN WAY OF LIFE IS DISAPPEARING BECAUSE THE GOVT. WON'T HELP OUT!!

WHAM

MY GOD... PEOPLE ARE HURTING OUT THERE.

"SLIDE-RULE AID."

YER IN A STEW, AREN'T YOU?

IT'S PLAINLY LABELED.

HEY... THE JOB OF VICE PRESIDENT IS CLEARLY UNDERRATED...

WHY DONCHA CALL UP THE MAN WHO FINALLY MADE THE OFFICE OF V.P. MEANINGFUL AND ASK HIM FOR ADVICE?...

WHADDYA MEAN NELSON ROCKEFELLER IS DEAD?

IT'S A CAMPAIGN CONTRIBUTION FROM THE UNITED COCAINE SMUGGLERS, PUSHERS AND AFFILIATED SCUM...

UH-OH.

"PLEASE ACCEPT THIS SMALL GIFT TO AID YOUR EFFORTS TOWARD VICTORY IN NOVEMBER!"

"...IN EXCHANGE, WE'D LIKE TO HAVE YOU SEE THAT ANOTHER $50 BILLION OF TAX MONEY BE SPENT ON STOPPING ANOTHER 1% OF ALL SMUGGLED DRUGS...

"LET'S KEEP THOSE COKE PRICES SHORED UP! OR WE'LL SHOOT YOU."

GOSH, I'VE ALWAYS BEEN UNCOMFORTABLE WITH GOVT. SUBSIDIES.

HOW'S LIFE, MR. CANDIDATE?

SWELL! WE GOT AN ENDORSEMENT FROM THE UNITED COCAINE SMUGGLERS, PUSHERS AND AFFILIATED SCUM.

PLUS, WE'RE BROKE, THE POLL RESULTS SMELL AND MY RUNNING MATE IS IN AN ALCOHOLIC COM—-ER... RELIGIOUS TRANCE.

MY CAMPAIGN IS IN TOTAL DISARRAY.

THIS... THIS IS THE MEDIA'S FAULT!!

CAMPAIGN IN CONFUSION.. POLLS PLUMMETING... DREAMS DRIBBLING DREARILY DOWN DA DRAIN..

DANDELIONS AHEAD

NO FUSSING ABOUT

SIGH.

KICK, KICK, KICK

BOB DOLE SHOULD'VE KNOWN ABOUT DANDELION PATCHES.

[147]

AS USUAL, WITHIN TWO WEEKS, A CLOUD OF CHAOS HAS DESCENDED UPON THE MIGHTY MEADOW PARTY POLITICAL MACHINE.

CANDIDATE MEDITATING FOR WORLD PEACE

BUT THERE IS DISTRESS AND SHAME ELSEWHERE ON THIS DEPRESSING DAWN...

Le Bloom Boarding Abode
MORAL VACANCY

ESPECIALLY IN THE ELEGANT SUITE OF THE DEEPLY DEMOCRATIC BINKLEYS...

I AM SO ASHAMED, SON...

I... I THINK JESSE JACKSON IS KINDA LOOPY.

WILLYA KEEP YER VOICE DOWN!

I ADMIT... JESSE CAN GIVE A HECK OF A SERMON... AND HE RHYMES WELL...

BUT I'M SORRY... I... I JUST DON'T SEE HIM AS THE LEADER OF THE FREE WORLD. PLEASE FORGIVE ME... PLEASE...

DAD! YOU'RE GOING FETAL WITH GUILT!

THAT'S IT... WE NEED PROFESSIONAL HELP!

HELLO?! DEMOCRAT CRISIS HOTLINE?!

GOD KNOWS, I CHERISH BLACK PEOPLE.

I CAME AS SOON AS I HEARD! HOW IS HE?!

HE'S HAVING A LIBERAL DEMOCRAT GUILT FIT!

HE FINALLY CONFRONTED THE FACT THAT HE DOESN'T WANT TO VOTE FOR JESSE. PLEASE TALK TO HIM.

POP... YOU REMEMBER OLIVER'S DAD, FRANK...

DAD!!

TOM! SPEAKING FOR BLACKS WORLD WIDE, WE DON'T HATE YOU!... TOM?

TOM... LISTEN... I... MYSELF... VOTED FOR AL HAIG LAST FEBRUARY. NOW CHILL OUT.

THE FIRST BLACK IN THE WHITE HOUSE WILL BE A CONSERVATIVE. IT'S JUST NOT OUR TURN THIS YEAR.

IT'S SOCIALLY OKAY TO DISLIKE JESSE, TOM.

REALLY?

REALLY.

CAN I LOATHE BILL COSBY AND HIS #★@!! PUDDING POPS?!

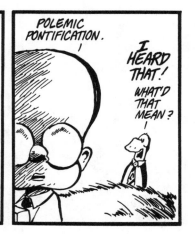

FINALLY.

A CANDIDATE EVERY AMERICAN CAN CALL THEIR OWN.

HE'S BEEN A HANDICAPPED UNIONIST MINORITY FARMER.

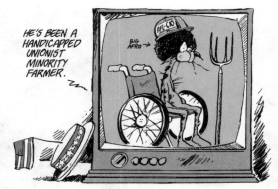

HE'S BEEN A RIGHT-WING, PRO-CHOICE, BORN-AGAIN SOUTHERN ELDERLY PROTECTIONIST PACIFIST.

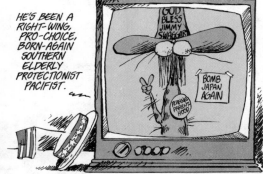

HE'S BEEN A REDNECK NORTHERN LIBERAL ETHNIC PRO-LIFE JEWISH FIXED-INCOME NO-NUKES GUN NUT.

AND HE'S BEEN A WOMAN NAMED FRIEDA.

BILL THE CAT FOR PRESIDENT

HE'S BEEN ONE OF US.

I KNOW YER IN THERE, MR. RELUCTANT V.P. CANDIDATE! SO GET BACK OUT HERE AND COLLECT SOME ENDORSEMENTS!

RATS.

THE NAME'S...ER, JOHN SMITH. I REPRESENT THE UNITED COCAINE PRODUCERS, SMUGGLERS, PUSHERS AND AFFILIATED SCUM.

CHARMED. SHALL WE STEP INTO THE PARLOR?

MR. CANDIDATE... WHAT IS YOUR POSITION ON TOUGH DRUG LAWS?

WELL.... I.. UH... UH... SUPPORT THEM.

GOOD!! NOTHING MAKES US MADDER THAN SOME LIBERAL TALKING DRUG LEGALIZATION!

WHY, WE'D ALL CLOSE DOWN WITHIN HOURS!! BURGLARY WOULD DROP 60%! MURDER, 70%! THE CITIES WOULD BE SAFE AGAIN!... POLICE... COAST GUARD... PRISON WORKERS... BILLIONAIRE DRUG CZARS... THERE'D BE LAYOFFS EVERYWHERE!!

GLAD TO HAVE YOU ON BOARD THE "TOUGH-ON-DRUGS" BANDWAGON!! WE'LL ANNOUNCE OUR ENDORSEMENT OF YOUR CANDIDACY IN A PRESS RELEASE!

GREAT.

I HATE SPECIAL-INTEREST GROUPS!!

SCRUB SCRUB

I **LIKE** COCKROACHES... I ESPECIALLY LIKE THE COCKROACH NAMED MILQUETOAST... IN FACT, WHEN I WAKE UP, I'M GONNA FETCH HIM A "DING DONG"...

FAT CHANCE, GREASY-FACE! I'LL HAVE YOU KNOW THAT FLIGHTLESS WATERFOWL ARE **HIGHLY RESISTANT** TO SUBLIMINAL SUGGESTION !!...

SNIFF.

A LOVELY "DING DONG"! TRULY! BUT WOULD YOU BE KIND ENUFF TO RUB IT AROUND THE GUNK UNDER THE FRIDGE A FEW TIMES?

..BUT NOT TO SHAMELESS MARTYRDOM.

COFFEE... NEED SOME COFFEE... JAVA...BLACK..

SNORT

PAPER... WHERE'Z THE PAPER...

icayune

★ CAMPAIGN WATCH
FROM THE LATEST BLOOM PICAYUNE HOLLYWOOD SQUARES POLL

↑ SPUDS MACKENZIE 47%
↑ GUMBY 13%
↑ RANDEE OF THE REDWOODS 9%
↑ BOZO 7%
↑ DUKAKIS 4.5%
↑ JACKSON 3%
↑ BUSH 2%
⇩ BILL 'N' OPUS -1% and dropping like a brick

WHO NEEDS CAFFEINE WHEN YA GOT THE MORNING POLLS?

OUR PRESIDENTIAL CANDIDATE DIDN'T COME HOME LAST NIGHT.

WENT ON A DATE WITH CORNELIA GUEST.

THE INTERNATIONAL DEBUTANTE?

ON THE BOUNCE FROM STALLONE.

CORNELIA AND BILL!

BILL 'N' CORNY!

THERE **IS** A SORT OF COSMIC HARMONY TO IT.

A REAL MEETING OF THE MINDS.

THIS IS CORNELIA GUEST'S MOTHER! IS MY LITTLE CORNY THERE?

SHE'S OUT DANCING WITH BILL THE CAT.

OH MY GOD. MY WORLD IS CRUMBLING ABOUT ME...

SHE **HAD** HIM !! SHE HAD STALLONE SIGNED, SEALED AND DELIVERED !! AND SHE LET HIM **SLIP AWAY** !!

AND WHO'S IT NOW? SOME OBSCENE-TONGUED CAT-BEAST! WHAT AM I SUPPOSED TO CALL ALL THIS?

SOCIAL CLIMBING.

BILL! STOP SHOOTING! JEANE KIRKPATRICK IS ON THE PHONE!!

PLEASE! SHE INSISTS ON TALKING TO YOU!

OH BILL...BILL! PLEASE STOP SHOOTING AT THE NEIGHBORS! WE'LL BE LIKE OLD TIMES! YOU'LL BE MY LITTLE CONTRA CASANOVA... AND ME, YOUR... YOUR... UH...

...HIS WHAT? "MUJAHEDDIN MAMA"? YEAH! GOOD!

POOR BILL THE CAT... ANOTHER OF SOCIETY'S OUTCASTS PUSHED INTO CRIMINAL ACTIVITY BY AN UNCARING AMERICA... BLAM! ZING! POLICE LINE

EDITOR'S NOTE:

TO BENEFIT THE OCCASIONAL READER OF THIS FEATURE, WE SHOULD EXPLAIN THAT THE MAN SHOWN HERE WAS ONCE A NEANDERTHAL CONSERVATIVE BEFORE BEING KIDNAPPED BY ALIENS WHO TRANSREVERSED HIS BRAIN. HE IS NOW A JACKSON PROGRESSIVE.

THUS THE IRONY.

continued—

I CERTAINLY HOPE OUR OPPRESSIVE SYSTEM WILL RESPECT THIS CRIMINAL'S RIGHTS! BLAM! BLAM!! ZING! ZING! POLICE LINE

FOR THE READERS WE NEVERTHELESS LOST BACK THERE — INCLUDING, AS USUAL, THE AUTHOR'S MOTHER, MARTHA JANE, 53... WE URGE ANOTHER REVIEW OF PANEL TWO.

TRUST US. IN CONTEXT, THIS ALL IS GLISTENING WITH COMIC IRONY.

—ed.

HOW ARE WE GONNA FACE TODAY'S PRESS CONFERENCE? WE NEED SOME SCANDAL CONTROL. LIKE THE JIM BAKKER METHOD. LYIN'. BILL BLASTS THE BEJEEZUS OUT OF EVERYTHING

OR THE JIMMY SWAGGART METHOD. CRYIN'.

MAYBE THE BILL CASEY METHOD. DYIN'? THINK OF ANOTHER APPROACH!

THE DEVIL MADE HIM DO IT. WE HAVE DOCUMENTS. FOR PRESIDENT

CALL MAKEUP. HIS NOSE IS SHINY. I'M TRYING. SIT UP STRAIGHT. OKAY... LISTEN—

WHAT WE WANT TO CAPTURE HERE IS YOUR COURAGE, MORAL CONVICTION, INTELLIGENCE, COMMUNICATIVE CONFIDENCE AND VISIONARY PHILOSOPHY.

HOW 'BOUT A LITTLE HINT OF HUMANITY? GOOD. AND WAVE.

OPUS →for VEEP←

LET'S BACK-LIGHT HIM.

F-22... 250TH

HE'S DROOLING! SPONGE MOP!!

OKAY. WHAT'RE WE TRYING TO CAPTURE HERE?

CONSCIOUSNESS.

C'MON, BILL BABY! PROJECT! POUT, BABY, POUT!

SHOOT! SHOOT!!

BILL

FOR PRESIDENT

A DESPERATE CHOICE FOR DESPERATE TIMES

LIFE IS NOT JOYFUL FOR A PRESIDENTIAL BACK-RUNNER. BUT SOMEWHERE... AT THIS VERY MOMENT... FORTUNES ARE CHANGING...

SCREEEEECH!!

The Bloom Picayune

SPUDS MACKENZIE IN DRUNKEN PILEUP WITH INNOCENT SAINT

INTOXICATED PRESIDENTIAL FRONT-RUNNER SMASHES INTO MOTHER TERESA'S VOLKSWAGEN

THIS IS, I BELIEVE, THE GRAND BULL-MOOSE GOLD-MEDAL WINNER OF MIXED BLESSINGS.

"CANDIDATE SPUDS MACKENZIE CAREENED INTO A CAR CARRYING MOTHER TERESA. SHE WAS BRUISED."

YEAH? YEAH?

"THE FAMED CORPORATE SPOKESMAN AND PRESIDENTIAL FRONT-RUNNER SHOWED A BLOOD-ALCOHOL LEVEL OF 92%."

OO!

"MOST SHOCKING OF ALL, WITNESSES REPORT HAVING SEEN MR. MACKENZIE DRINK 17 CASES OF..."

WHAT? WHAT?

"...HEINEKEN."

WE HAVE A SCANDAL.

YEAH

TONIGHT: FURTHER REVELATIONS REGARDING CANDIDATE SPUDS MACKENZIE:

PUBLIC AGGRESSIVENESS...

MR. SPUDS.. DON'T YOU THINK—

GIMME ANOTHA SHOT BEFORE I RIP OUT THAT GROUND BEEF YOU CALL A BRAIN AND EAT IT FOR LUNCH!

A DRINKING PROBLEM OF PREVIOUSLY UNSUSPECTED PROPORTIONS...

Bud Light

GLUB GLUB GLUB GLUB

AND RUMORS OF UNPRESIDEN-TIAL ANTISOCIAL BEHAVIOR...

LOOK! I'M A "COPPERTONE" AD!!

MILO! BEFORE WE GO TO WORK...TELL ME IF MY NOSE HAS SHRUNK ANY!

Picayune NewsRoom

PFFT

FACTS

SORRY.

DRAT. I THOUGHT THAT MIGHT BE ONE OF THE MANY SIDE BENEFITS OF BEING A SMOKER.

POOF

FACTS

YEAH? NAME JUST ONE.

WELL...WE SORTA SMELL LIKE HUMPHREY BOGART.

FACTS

HE'S BEEN DEAD FOR THIRTY YEARS!!

EXACTLY.

FACTS

I'D LIKE TO PLACE AN AD.

PUFF PUFF PUFF

Personals

"WHITE SINGLE WOMAN, 27 ISH, KNOCKOUT... SEEKS SHORT, BLOBBISH MATE. BIG NOSE OKAY."

"...MUST BE SWEET, NAIVE. POLITICAL ASPIRATIONS A PLUS. BOW TIES A REAL TURN-ON..."

"NO SMOKERS."

"...NO SMOKERS."

NO CIGARETTES TODAY?

QUIT COLD PUFFIN.

"TURKEY."

I THOUGHT I'D BETTER FIND A BAD HABIT SOMEWHAT MORE SOCIALLY ACCEPTABLE THAN SMOKING...

LIKE RINSING SOCKS IN A DRINKING FOUNTAIN OR IMITATING BODY NOISES IN A CROWDED ELEVATOR.

YEAH.

SOMETHING'S WRONG... WHAT'S WRONG?

AN EMERGENCY TENANTS' MEETING HAS BEEN CALLED AT THE BOARDINGHOUSE.

THIS JUNE 20TH, THE SUPREME COURT RULED THAT "MALE ONLY" CLUBS ARE UNCONSTITUTIONAL...

WELL NOTHING'S MORE "MALE ONLY" THAN "BLOOM COUNTY"! WE'VE GOT TO INTRODUCE A WOMAN!!

WE'RE SO SORRY.

WHAT'S NEXT? UNISEX UNDERWEAR? PHYLLIS SCHLAFLY WAS RIGHT!

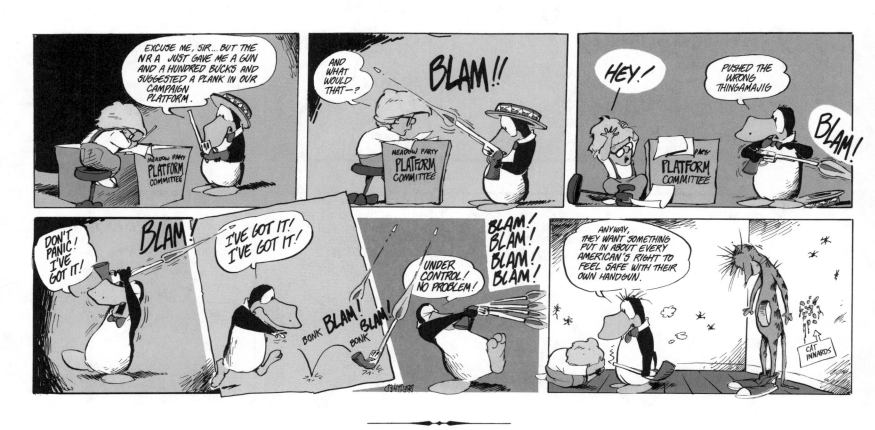

WOMEN. LIVING HERE. I DON'T KNOW...

THEY SEEM TO MAKE IT THEIR MISSION IN LIFE TO MAKE ALL MEN LOOK LIKE TOTAL TWITS.

BINKLEY! WHERE DID YOU GET SUCH A SKEWERED VIEW OF... UH...

MY GOD. YOU'VE BEEN READING THE COMICS PAGE.

YEAH.

I PLACED THE AD, SIR.

WHERE?

IT'S CIRCLED. I WROTE IT MYSELF.

Personals

NUDE CHICKENS

All types. $14.95. $16.95 with dewlap. Mailed discreetly in plain brown paper. Must be 62 or over... evenings.

WOMAN WANTED

To join all-male ensemble. Age 5 to 90. Should provide own linens. Must not make men look like twits. 555-43...

LOOKS GOOD.

I LIKE THE "TWITS" PART.

AH... MAKING SPECIAL ACCOMMODATIONS FOR THE IMMINENT FEMININE PRESENCE, EH?

YOU BETCHA.

BATHROOM OCCUPIED DO NOT...

THAT'S VERY CHIVALROUS OF YOU.

CHIVALROUS?

BATHROOM OCCUPIED DO NOT BARGE IN

BATHROOM OCCUPIED DO NOT BARGE IN

THIS IS FOR ME, TWEEDLE-DUMB.

BATHROOM OCCUPIED DO NOT BARGE IN

THE VARIOUS MALES OF BLOOM COUNTY DREAM OF THE IDEAL FEMALE THEY HOPE WILL JOIN THEIR WORLD SOON.

FIRST... THE ELDER BINKLEY:

SNORE...

HI, TOM... IT'S ME, YOUR ALL-TIME ULTIMATE DREAM WIFE!

HAIR BY T. RICHARD.

YOU'VE GOT TO BE KIDDING.

OH, C'MON... REMEMBER WHERE YOU FIRST SAW ME?

MAKEUP BY GIORGIO. SUIT BY ZELDA SWIMWEAR OF NEW YORK.

UH... CHURCH PICNIC?

NOT QUITE!

SPORTS ILLUSTRATED

WOW! SWIM 88!!

BINKLEY SR. IS DREAMING...

I'M SO ASHAMED! I'M TOO MATURE TO THINK OF A "SPORTS ILLUSTRATED" BIMBETTE AS MY WIFELY IDEAL!

BUT AS YOUR *IDEAL*, I'M NOT JUST A BIMBETTE...

I'M A PERFECT MOTHER, A GREAT COOK AND ALMOST BUT NOT QUITE AS BRIGHT AND WITTY AS YOU ARE!

...AND YOU LOOK LIKE BROOKE SHIELDS.

..WITH BIG GARBANZOS!

DAD!

BINKLEY! WHAT ARE YOU DOING IN MY DREAM?

I WANTED TO MEET THIS "ULTIMATE, IDEAL WIFE-WOMAN" YOU'VE BEEN TELLING ME I SHOULD BE LOOKING FOR ALL THESE YEARS!

YEAH... RIGHT. UH...

OH, HECK... SON, MEET ELEANOR ROOSEVELT.

HEY!

THE NEWLY FEMINIST STEVE DALLAS DREAMS OF *HIS* IDEAL WOMAN...

HI, STEVE... IT'S ME!

I'M TOUGH AND AGGRESSIVE AND GO TO WORK EACH DAY TO COMPETE WITH MEN ON MY OWN UNCOMPROMISING TERMS.

THEN I COME HOME TO MY HUSBAND...

...AND LOUNGE AROUND IN "LITTLE FRENCH MAID" LINGERIE.

HEY! ONLY IF YOU WOULD'VE ANYWAY...

STEVE'S IDEAL...

..AND SO THEY GAVE ME THE GM ACCOUNT AND I OPTIONED 300 SHARES ON MARGIN WITH--

SAY, DREAM WIFE...YOU SURE YOU DON'T MIND MASSAGING MY FEET?

NOW STEVE... YOU KNOW WHAT FEMINISM IS ALL ABOUT...

THE RIGHT TO MAKE *CHOICES!*

GOOD. AS LONG AS THAT'S UNDERSTOOD. S'POSE YOU MIGHT CHOOSE TO RUB A LITTLE HARDER?

SURE, BUBBA.

[169]

SPUDS MACKENZIE HERE. AND YOU'RE –?
OPUS.
WANNA BEER, OTIS?
NO, THANK YOU.
SAY.. I DROPPED BY TO DISCUSS THIS BUSINESS ABOUT A LACK OF FEMALES AROUND BLOOM COUNTY... IT'S ALL A CROCK, YA KNOW.
I SEE.
SURE YA DON'T WANNA BEER? ..FLUSHES OUT THE OL' PLUMBING LIKE "TY-D-BOL."
OO.
—CONTINUED!

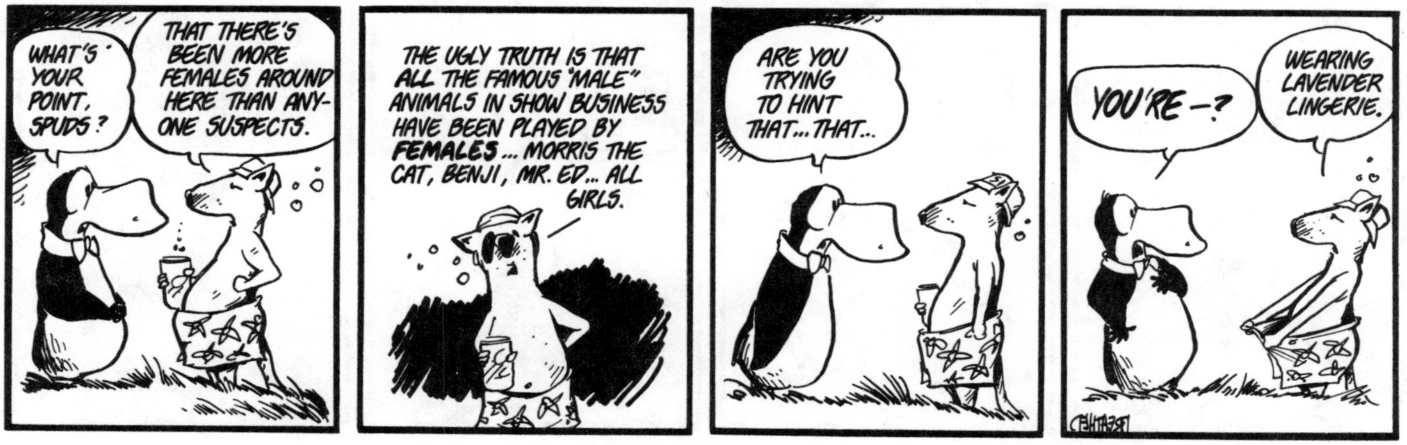
WHAT'S YOUR POINT, SPUDS?
THAT THERE'S BEEN MORE FEMALES AROUND HERE THAN ANYONE SUSPECTS.
THE UGLY TRUTH IS THAT ALL THE FAMOUS "MALE" ANIMALS IN SHOW BUSINESS HAVE BEEN PLAYED BY FEMALES... MORRIS THE CAT, BENJI, MR. ED... ALL GIRLS.
ARE YOU TRYING TO HINT THAT... THAT...
YOU'RE –?
WEARING LAVENDER LINGERIE.

SPUDS MACKENZIE IS A HER!!
CAT'S OUTTA THE BAG!
YEAH, BENEATH THIS FALSE HOLLYWOOD IMAGE BEATS THE SENSITIVE HEART OF A FEMALE...
AND LIKE ALL DAMES, MY INHIBITIONS DROP LIKE LEAD WHEN I GET SAUCED...
UH-OH.
SO WHADYA SAY, SQUAT, DARK AND HANDSOME... BUY A GIRL A DRINK?

MR. ED, BENJI, MORRIS, CHEETAH THE CHIMP... RIN TIN TIN, GENTLE BEN, FLIPPER... ME... ALL MALE ANIMAL STARS PLAYED IN REALITY BY FEMALES...
MILK
AND THERE'S ONE MORE! A VEERRRRY FAMILIAR FACE RIGHT HERE IN BLOOM COUNTY! KNOW WHO IT IS?
WHO?
BONK!
BOTH YOU AND I KNOW THAT SHE'S NOT GOING TO WAKE UP UNTIL THAT LAST STATEMENT HAS WREAKED TOTAL PANDEMONIUM AROUND HERE.
SNORE

ACTUALLY, I RACE OFFSHORE SPEED-BOATS IN MY SPARE TIME. ALSO—

WAIT! I KNOW THAT VOICE!

SINGLES PARTY LINE

I'M SURE YOU DON'T, MISS.

YES! YOU'RE THAT FAT LITTLE GUY ON WALNUT STREET WHO'S ALWAYS PICKING HIS TOES!

SLAM !!

REALITY HAS NO BUSINESS IN AFFAIRS OF THE HEART.

IT'S THE PHONE BILL WITH ALL MY "PARTY LINE" CALLS ON IT.

RIP!

YEEAIGH !!

BWOING!

DO YOU ALL HAVE ANY IDEA HOW PAINFUL THAT SORT OF THING IS?

AS INEVITABLE AS RAGWEED POLLEN, THE SEASON'S FIRST REAL CONTROVERSY DESCENDED UPON THE MEADOWCRATS...

SIGH...

BILL

MEADOWCRATS HEADQUARTERS

THE PRESS HAD DISCOVERED WHAT THEIR CANDIDATE HAD DONE DURING THE DARK YEARS OF VIETNAM...

The Bloom Picayune

BILL INSISTS: "I WAS D***** PROUD TO SERVE IN THE CANADIAN NATIONAL MOOSE MOUNTIES!"

"At least I wasn't a draft dodger" says cat

THE CANDIDATE IN 1969

PARTY INSIDERS HUDDLE TO DECIDE HOW BEST TO HANDLE THE FUSS OVER THEIR CANDI-DATE'S PAST DRAFT AVOIDANCE...

OKAY, THEN... WE LIE, DISTORT AND THROW BLAME.

HOW 'BOUT THIS: WE APPEAL TO THE MATURITY OF THE AMERICAN VOTER AND ADDRESS THE ISSUE WITH DISARMING CANDOR.

BILL '88

NAH.

YES, BILL JOINED THE CANADIAN NATIONAL MOOSE MOUNTIES IN 1969... ARE YOU SUGGESTING THAT THIS WAS A HYPOCRITICAL ACT FOR A HAWKISH RIGHT-WINGER?

WHY, THERE WERE MOOSE ENEMIES ALL AROUND... NAZI MOOSE... COMMIE MOOSE... IT WAS... UH, YOU KNOW...

...FRIGHTFUL.

AS ANOTHER GREAT WARRIOR ONCE SAID, WE MAY BE IN DEEP DOO-DOO.

BILL! LISTEN! ARE THERE ANY MORE SKELETONS IN YOUR CLOSET?

IS THERE ANYTHING WE OVERLOOKED THAT WOULD KEEP YOU FROM BEING AN EFFECTIVE PRESIDENT?

COMATOSE.

..UGLY QUIRKS? LITTLE PERSONALITY FAULTS? NOTHING?

BRAIN DEAD. LAZY. EASILY CONFUSED.

WE STILL HAVE A WINNER!

FOLLOWS ASTROLOGY. NAPS FREQUENTLY.

RONALD-ANN KNOWS A BETTER YEAR IS AROUND THE CORNER BECAUSE IT'S ON THE WIND LIKE PERFUME...

HOPE... HARMONY... HAPPINESS... HERRING HEADS...

SNIFF

EXCUSE ME...

DON'T SAY IT. AM I UPWIND AGAIN, MADAM?

I'VE GONE AND MADE YOU FEEL BAD ABOUT YOURSELF.

WHAT'S WORSE THAN SMELLING LIKE HERRING HEADS.?

THERE'S LOTS OF THINGS WORSE, OPUS!

YEAH? LIKE WHAT?

YOU COULD BE A WALRUS AND SMELL LIKE PENGUIN HEADS.

FEEL BETTER?

BOY, WE ALL KNOW HOW AWFUL THAT SMELLS, DON'T WE?

IT STARTED SO INNOCENTLY!

MR. JONES, WE'RE FROM THE ANIMAL RIGHTS LEAGUE.

WE'VE HEARD THAT THERE ARE EXPERIMENTS GOING ON IN THIS HOUSE WHICH INVOLVE AN ANIMAL BEING TREATED LESS THAN LOVINGLY.

HUG A COCKROACH

HERE? THIS HOUSE? YOU MEAN, LIKE, BEHIND THESE WALLS? WITHOUT ME KNOWING? IMPOSSIBLE. GOOD DAY!

OLIVER WENDELL JONES..!!

BUSY.

CAT SWEAT

SON... WHAT ARE YOU DOING IN THE BASEMENT?

TRYING TO EXTRACT SWEAT FROM A CAT.

I BELIEVE A REVOLUTIONARY NEW UNDERARM DEODORANT CAN BE DERIVED FROM THE ENZYMES OF FELINE SWEAT.

AH. DEODORANT RESEARCH. WELL, AS LONG AS SOCIETY BENEFITS SIGNIFICANTLY, FINE.

425,000 RESEARCH CRITTERS ARE SENT TO THE GREAT TEST LAB IN THE SKY EACH DAY FOR SIMILAR BENEFITS.

RUMBLING GUILT PANGS

I'VE TRIED EVERYTHING. I CAN'T GET OUR LAB ANIMAL TO SWEAT.

LEMME TRY.

OKAY, BILLY BOY... LISTEN CAREFULLY:

CAT SWEAT

PRESIDENT QUAYLE! AAIGH!

HE'S SWEATING.

I'M SWEATING.

CAT SWEAT

FRONT AND CENTER, MISTER PRODUCT-DEVELOPMENT GENIUS..!!

LAST NIGHT I TRIED YOUR DEODORANT MADE FROM CAT-SWEAT ENZYMES...

"GOOD HOUSEKEEPING"'S NOT GONNA GO FOR THIS.

FETCH ME THE WEED KILLER.

I'VE GOT YOUR SHARE OF THE FIRST WEEK'S PROFITS.

MINUS UTILITIES, LABOR, CATERING, RAW MATERIALS, GAS, BUG SPRAY, BONUSES AND "EXTRANEOUS OVERHEAD." LEAVING YOU...

A DIME.

I UNDERSTAND HOLLYWOOD WORKS ALONG THESE LINES.

IT WAS A WEEK LATER WHEN ONE OF THE MOST AVID CONSUMERS OF THE MIRACLE CAT-SWEAT SCALP TONIC FINALLY NOTICED.

ACK ACK ACK ACK ACK ACK ACK ACK ACK

THERE WERE SLIGHT BUT SOCIALLY INCONVENIENT SIDE EFFECTS.

OLIVER WENDELL JONES ?!!

LADIES AND GENTLEMEN... THE SURGEON GENERAL OF THE UNITED STATES:

SPECIAL REPORT

SHIP OVERNIGHT

DUE TO REPORTS OF RUDE "ACK"ING SIDE EFFECTS, DR. OLIVER'S CAT-SWEAT SCALP TONIC IS NOW CONSIDERED A CONTROLLED SUBSTANCE... ILLEGAL TO OWN OR SELL.

NO SMOKIN DAMMI

WE HOPE THIS DOESN'T PROVE AN INCONVENIENCE. GOOD NIGHT AND GOOD HEALTH.

TONIC
SCALP TONIC
SCALP TONIC
LP NIC
DR. SCALP TONIC

GIMME A BOTTLE OF THAT BALDNESS CURE!

CAN'T. IT'S A CONTROLLED SUBSTANCE.

Dr. Oliver's SCALP CLOSED 10¢

HERE'S A BUCK!

SIR... IT'S ILLEGAL

Dr. Oliver's SCALP TONIC CLOSED

FIVE BUCKS!

YOU DON'T UNDERSTAND... YOU'D BE BREAKING A CONGRESSIONALLY MANDATED U.S. LAW. ...OBVIOUSLY UNTHINKABLE.

Dr. OLIVER'S HAIR

TEN GRAND!!

DOES IT SAY "TEN CENTS" ON THE SIGN, OR AM I LOOPY?

Dr. Oliver's SCALP CLOSED 10¢

BILL, ON BEHALF OF THE NOW-DEFUNCT CORPORATION, WE'D LIKE TO SAY THANKS FOR BEING TORTURED.

CAT SWEAT

YOUR PAINFULLY EXTRACTED SWEAT EARNED US $52 MILLION... ALL NOW WELL INVESTED.

YOU DID INVEST IT, DIDN'T YOU, MR. COMPANY ACCOUNTANT?

IN A MANNER OF SPEAKING.

CHECK FOR $52 MILLION!

PEOPLE FOR THE ETHICAL TREATMENT OF ANIMALS

A CONSUMER FOLLOW-UP ON THE LONG-TERM RESULTS OF DR. OLIVER'S CAT-SWEAT SCALP TONIC AND HAIR RESTORER:

AH... AAH...

AAH... CHOO!!

YOUR DAD'S WHAT, OLIVER?

ON THE FLOOR SOBBING AND SUCKING HIS THUMB.

NOW OLIVER... YOUR FATHER HAS SUDDENLY GONE WHAT?

SPEAR BALD.

DUE TO A DARK AND SINISTER FORCE IN THE UNIVERSE KNOWN AS WHAT?

HIS SON.

WHICH, AS FAR AS HE IS CONCERNED, PROVIDES LEGAL GROUNDS FOR WHAT?

TRADING ME IN TOWARD A PET GERBIL.

NOW WE'RE COMMUNICATING!

"OCCUPANT"... "OCCUPANT"... "OCCUPANT"... "OCCUPANT"...

"OCCUPANT"... "OCCUPANT"...

SHEESH!

WE'VE BECOME SUCH A DEPERSONALIZED SOCIETY!

HERE'S ONE: "MOTHERLESS OCCUPANT SUFFERING OEDIPUS COMPLEX — SHORT, DARK, NOSE HEMORRHOIDS."

OH, THAT'S ME!

THE FREE WORLD'S MOST BITTERSWEET CHRISTMAS STORY IS ABOUT TO BEGIN WITH A YELLOWING NEWS CLIPPING SENT TO OPUS FROM "THE ANTARCTIC GAZETTE"...

MOM!

Oct. 3, 1987
HEROINE PENGUIN OF FALKLAND WAR FOUND ALIVE AFTER FIVE YEARS
SOLD TO U.S. COSMETICS TESTING LAB

SHE WASN'T DEAD!

SHE ISN'T DEAD!!

WHO?! WHAT? THE DEMOCRATIC PARTY?!

IT WAS TRUE. OPUS'S MOTHER MIGHT INDEED BE ALIVE... BUT FIRST — SOME HISTORY:

YES! GOOD! TELL THEM WHILE I PACK!

APRIL 1982. THE FALKLAND ISLANDS... A DESPERATE YOUNG MOTHER RUSHES HER HATCHLING SON ONTO A SHIP BOUND FOR AMERICA WHILE THE WINDS OF WAR STIR EVER CLOSER.

AMERICA HANDLE W/ CARE

LEGEND WILL LATER SPEAK OF THE 73 BRITISH AND ARGENTINE SAILORS SAVED BY A VALIANT AVIAN DELIVERESS...

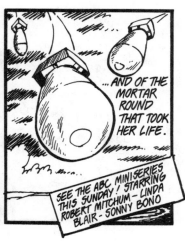

...AND OF THE MORTAR ROUND THAT TOOK HER LIFE.

SEE THE ABC MINISERIES THIS SUNDAY! STARRING ROBERT MITCHUM - LINDA BLAIR - SONNY BONO

THE INFANT OPUS WAS TO EVENTUALLY LAND UPON THE HOPEFUL SHORES OF BLOOM COUNTY. THIS WAS HOME NOW.

FRESH MEAT KEEP REFRIGERATED

YEARS LATER HE WOULD JOURNEY BACK TO THE SOUTH ATLANTIC SEARCHING FOR THE MOTHER HE NEVER KNEW...

...AND NEVER WOULD.

The MARTYR OF THE FALKLANDS 1964-1982 SHE LOVED HER BOY

BUT WAIT! DID SHE ACTUALLY SURVIVE?! IS SHE IMPRISONED SOMEWHERE EVEN AS WE SPEAK?

YES! YES!!

JUST LIKE A SHIRLEY TEMPLE MOVIE!!

MOM QUEST II

DON'T TRY TO TALK ME OUT OF IT, MILO!!
MY MOTHER IS BEING HELD IN A PRODUCT-TESTING LAB SOMEWHERE AND I'M GONNA FIND HER!!

OR AM I SETTING MYSELF UP FOR A GIANT DISAPPOINTMENT?

WHAT IF SHE'S MORE LIKE NANCY REAGAN THAN JUNE LOCKHART? WHAT IF SHE'S NOT COMPASSIONATE? WHAT IF SHE EATS COCKROACHES?

OOO... GROSS... THPPFT.

JUST DON'T TRY TO TALK ME OUT OF IT, MILO!

OKAY.

GANGWAY! COMING THROUGH! EMERGENCY!!

MY MOTHER MAY BE ALIVE AND KEPT CAPTIVE AT A COSMETICS-TESTING LAB.!!

BUMMER.

BUT THEN MY MOTHER FELL INTO A BAG OF FLOUR AND DIED AS AN EGG McMUFFIN.

STRICTLY A FANCIFUL JEST! —Legal dept.

SO MOM'S AT A PRODUCT-TESTING LAB, EH? GOSH... I ALWAYS IMAGINED WHAT GOES ON IN THOSE PLACES.....

TRY SOME NEW SHAVING CREAM, FLUFFY!

OKEY-DOKEY!

GILLETTE CO.

WELL? SMOOTH AND CREAMY?

IT KINDA TICKLES MY NOSE! =GIGGLE!=

GILLETTE CO.

MAN AND CRITTERS WORKIN' TOGETHER! IT'S SO... CHRISTMAS!

HELLO! COULD YOU PLEASE DIRECT ME--

ARE YOU ONE OF THOSE ANIMAL-RIGHTS NUTS?!

Gillette
Colgate
Clorox
Dow Cl
Clairol,
Faberg
Bristol
Procter
Revlon.

ME?! I'M JUST LOOKING FOR MY MOTHER... AND IF YOU COULD--

DON'T THROW BLOOD ON ME!!

I JUST DO MY JOB! MY WORK IS IMPORTANT! I LIKE MYSELF! I'M SURE I DO!!

I CAN'T HELP YOU.

EXTREMISM CAN MAKE THINGS SO INCONVENIENT.

ANIMAL TESTING ROOM

NO SCREAMING ALLOWED DURING LUNCH

EXCUSE ME... UH, MISTER "TWELVE"... I WONDER IF YOU'VE SEEN... ER...

SAY, WHAT ARE YOU DOING?

ME?

WHY, I'M LYING IN STOCKS TO KEEP ME FROM CLAWING MY EYEBALL OUT OF MY LIDS THAT THEY CLIPPED OPEN AFTER SQUIRTING IN THE OVEN CLEANER.

THEN I GUESS YOU HAVEN'T SEEN MUCH OF ANYTHING LATELY, HUH?

NO. WHY? BARBARA BUSH DYE HER HAIR?

I'D LIKE TO SEE THAT!

AS I HAVE RECENTLY BEEN ASSAULTED BY THE ATHEISTS AND UNGENTLEMANLY PERSONS RESPONSIBLE FOR THIS "COMIC"...

IT IS ONLY FAIR TO SHOW THE FOLLOWING SECRET FILM OF ANIMAL TESTING PER-FORMED BY THE BLOOM COUNTY CARTOON CO. *ITSELF.*

ROLL IT.

OKAY, GROUP... HOW 'BOUT THIS ONE ?

HA! HA! HA!

HEE! HEE!

GIGGLE!

GOOD. AND HOW ABOUT...

...THIS ONE ?

YEEEAUGCH!

NEEDS EDITING.

I GUESS WE KNOW WHO'S *REALLY* SLAUGHTERING BUNNIES AROUND HERE, DON'T WE ?

THEY'RE ONLY *LIGHTLY STUNNED!*

BOY! THAT WAS A STINKER!

DO YOU THINK I *DON'T* WANT FRIENDS ? DO YOU THINK I DON'T *WANT* TO BE LIKED ?

WE'RE ALL RIDING TOGETHER ON THIS SPACESHIP CALLED EARTH... WE'D BETTER DARN WELL LEARN TO LIKE EACH OTHER...

IT'S A LONELY TREK THROUGH THIS VEIL OF TEARS WE CALL LIFE...

AND LET ME TELL YOU SOMETHING, PILGRIMS... NO COCKROACH IS AN ISLAND UNTO HIMSELF!!

MILQUETOAST

CLICK!

MILQUETOAST

GOOD EVENING, MRS. LINDERWÜRST! BY THE BY, DEAR... JUST HOW IS A CHAP S'POSED TO FIND A COZY PLACE TO CURL UP IN AT NIGHT IF YOU DON'T START TRIMMING THAT NOSTRIL HAIR ?

ZING! ZING! ZING! ZING!

MRS. LINDERWÜRST: CLEARLY AN ISLAND UNTO *HERSELF!!*

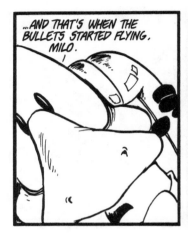

THORNHUMP HERE, WITH A FRIENDLY *SALUTE* TO THE CRAYOLA CRAYON COMPANY !!

BLOOM COUN ♥s CRAYOLA

...WHICH WAS ACCIDENTALLY MENTIONED HERE AS SELLING RACIALLY INSENSITIVE PINK CRAYONS LABELED "FLESH"...

BLOOM COUNTY ♥s CRAYOLA

...A GRAVE AND FOOLISH MISTAKE. CRAYOLA HASN'T HAD "FLESH" SINCE 1963.

IT *DOES* HAVE "INDIAN RED," THO.

WE ALSO SALUTE CRAYOLA'S FORGIVING LAWYERS !

S'POSE THEY HAVE "NEGRO BROWN—"..?

OW!

JAB!

BLOOM COUN ♥s CRAYOLA

1988... A GOOD YEAR.

WOULD YOU HAVE DONE ANYTHING DIFFERENT?

NOT A THING.

ME NEITHER.

I'D DO EVERYTHING EXACTLY THE SAME.

ME TOO.

EXACTLY.

ACTUALLY, I WOULDN'T HAVE MY NOSE FAT LIPOSUCTIONED OUT, COLLAPSING THE SUPERSTRUCTURE INTO A "Q-TIP"-LIKE SHAPE AGAIN!

...AND ALSO I WOULDN'T HAVE RUN FOR VICE PRESIDENT. I GUESS.

SO, IN HINDSIGHT, YOU WOULD HAVE DONE *EVERYTHING* DIFFERENTLY LAST YEAR ?

YES.

AND IN NEXT YEAR'S HINDSIGHT, YOU'LL REGRET EVERYTHING YOU DID *THIS* YEAR ?

I THINK SO.

SOME OF US LIVE IN PERPETUAL 20-20 CHAOS.

THE FIRST SNOW OF 1989 !

SSSSSSS

AAUGH!

ACID SNOW!!

DON'T WORRY, KIDS! IT'S JUST A SPECIAL EFFECT FOR EFFECT !

"BACTINE," PLEASE.

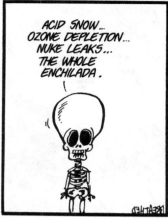

FACT: DONALD TRUMP WAS HIT BY HIS OWN ANCHOR LAST WEEK.

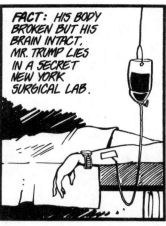

FACT: HIS BODY BROKEN BUT HIS BRAIN INTACT, MR. TRUMP LIES IN A SECRET NEW YORK SURGICAL LAB.

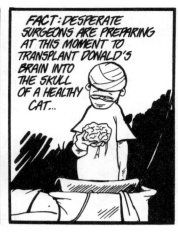

FACT: DESPERATE SURGEONS ARE PREPARING AT THIS MOMENT TO TRANSPLANT DONALD'S BRAIN INTO THE SKULL OF A HEALTHY CAT...

FACT: IT ISN'T HEATHCLIFF.

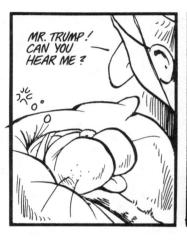

MR. TRUMP! CAN YOU HEAR ME?

HUH? WHA—... WHERE AM I?

YOU WERE HIT BY AN ANCHOR. WE PUT YOUR BRAIN IN A CAT.

I... I'M IN A CAT?

YES, SIR.

THE CATSKILLS? KATMANDU? CAT STEVENS?...

NO... NO... NO...

SO I'M A CAT NOW, EH, DOC?

IT WAS ALL WE COULD DO, MR. TRUMP.

AS YOU KNOW, I'M QUITE A PHILOSOPHER...

...AND ON THE GREAT LEDGER SHEET OF LIFE, I SHOULD LIST THE ASSETS OF THIS SITUATION...

EXACTLY!

LEGALLY, I CAN POOP IN ED KOCH'S FLOWER BED.

KNOCK KNOCK

OH, IVANA! IT'S ME... DONALD!

DARLING!

AAIGH!!

IT'S A LONG STORY... BUT IT'S ME! REALLY! I'LL PROVE IT:

♪ "WHO'S MY LITTLE MISS GOLDIKNOCKERS?"...

SHE USED TO GIGGLE WHEN I SAID THAT.

Today is the birthday of America's premier poet, Emily Dickinson. As an affectionate tribute, we offer the following dramatization of one of her lesser-known works:

Do*
by Emily Dickinson

* From *The Other Poems of Emily Dickinson*, edited by William Phillips : Andrews and McMeel, Inc., Copyright 1883, 1889, 1890

Do run through gilded veld with sunshine fluster...

Do lean to norther' wind of Autumn bluster.

Do dance 'pon emerald pond of winter crusted...

Do waltz in morning's dawn butterfly trusted!

Do taste moonbeams crossing all starlight dusted...

Just don't sneeze while flossing that upper cuspid.

THAT'S THE MOST ADORABLE LITTLE COLORED GIRL PLAYING OUTSIDE.

"COLORED"? YOU'RE SAYING "COLORED PEOPLE" IN 1988? YOU KNOW BETTER, MA.

THEN WHY THE "NATIONAL ASSOCIATION FOR THE ADVANCEMENT OF COLORED PEOPLE"? I DON'T THINK NEGROES MIND AT ALL.

DON'T SAY "NEGROES," MA! YOU CAN'T SAY "NEGROES"!

CAN I SAY "UNITED NEGRO COLLEGE FUND"?

YOU ARE BAITING ME, MA!

THAT'S IT. WE'RE LEAVING.

STAY PUT, REGINALD. "MISTER SOCIALLY SENSITIVE" ISN'T THROUGH SHAMING HIS PARENTS INTO ENLIGHTENMENT.

EVERYBODY JUST CALM DOWN. LET'S AGREE TO USE THE NEW-AGE TERM "PEOPLE OF COLOR."

PEOPLE OF COLOR.

PEOPLE OF COLOR.

COLORED PEOPLE.

NO!!

WE'RE LEAVING.

STARTING NOW, NO MORE ANIMALISTICALLY EXPLOITIVE HABITS FOR ME.

MUNCH MUNCH MUNCH...

NO EATIN' PORK, CHICKEN, BEEF, FISH, DAIRY PRODUCTS OR VEAL. ESPECIALLY VEAL.

VEAL'S BAD.

REAL BAD.

NO FUR!...LEATHER! IVORY! WOOL! DOWN COATS! NOR EEL-SKIN COWBOY BOOTS!

UH-UH.

...NO MOUSE TRAPS... AND NOOOOOO FLY SWATTERS.

RIGHT!

I AM AT ONENESS WITH ALL MY BROTHERS ON THIS SPACESHIP EARTH!

AMEN!

EXCEPT FOR STUPID COCKROACHES!

WOMP!

WOMP!

WOMP!

MORAL FAILURES CAN BE SUCH A BUMMER.

BROTHER, YOU'RE ON MY WIENER.

SPEAKING OF COCKROACHES, THE FOLLOWING IS A "BLOOM COUNTY" NATURE DOCUMENTARY: "THE SECRET NIGHTLIFE OF THE COMMON HOUSE ROACH"

PARTY TIME!

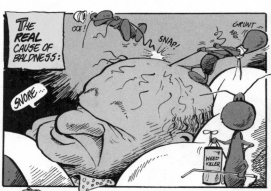

THE REAL CAUSE OF BALDNESS:

OOF!

SNAP!

GRUNT

SNORE...

WEED KILLER

THOSE NIGHTLY 3 A.M. BABY TANTRUMS EXPLAINED:

"BIG BIRD" JUST GOT SUCKED INTO THE ENGINE OF A B-1 BOMBER!

WAAAA!

THE SUBCONSCIOUS SOURCE OF WHITE AMERICA'S GENERAL TASTE IN THINGS:

PSST! PEE-WEE HERMAN IS ENDLESSLY HILARIOUS!

THE SOULFUL ALLURE OF RAP MUSIC CONTINUES TO ESCAPE YOU.

TACO BELL! MM-MMM GOOD!

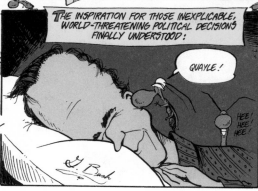

THE INSPIRATION FOR THOSE INEXPLICABLE, WORLD-THREATENING POLITICAL DECISIONS FINALLY UNDERSTOOD:

QUAYLE!

HEE! HEE! HEE!

G. Bush

EXPLAINS JUST ONE HECK OF A LOT, DON'T IT?

THPPT!

YA KNOW... SOMETIMES I THINK ABOUT THOSE HUGE PILES OF MONEY I HAVE...

YEAH?

...AND THEN I LOOK AT THE VAST WEALTH WITHIN THE BEAUTY OF THAT DAFFODIL...

YEAH! YEAH!

MY GOD...

YES!

I SHOULD BUY A HUMONGOUS NURSERY!

NO! AARGH...

DONNA REED?

MARILYN QUAYLE.

I'D LIKE TO APOLOGIZE FOR YESTERDAY'S WHOLLY UNSANCTIONED SATIRICAL ATTACK ON THE VICE PRESIDENT'S LOVELY WIFE.

W.A. THORNHUMP
C.E.O., BLOOM COUNTY, INC.

BAD PENGUIN! BAD, BAD PENGUIN! NAUGHTY PENGUIN!!

OBVIOUSLY, HE WAS UNAWARE THAT THE CARTOON TAX BILL IS UP FOR PRESIDENTIAL VETO THIS WEEK... HA! HA!

WHO AM I? MARILYN QUAYLE OR MARY TYLER MOORE IN 1962?

BAD PENGUIN! IMPOLITIC PENGUIN!

DON'T HANG UP ON ME AGAIN, IVANA! IT'S ME... YOUR DONALD!

THAT'S RIGHT... I'M A PENNILESS CAT NOW... BUT I'M STILL ME!...

LESS ABOUT $600 MILLION.

... AREN'T I JUST AS LOVABLE A GUY WITHOUT THE $600 MIL?!

OR IS THAT A STUPID QUESTION?

MUNCH MUNCH CHEW CHOMP SNORT

MOVIE BUFFS: ANY OF THIS LOOK FAMILIAR?

UGH! TURNIPS!... I'VE BEEN FORCED TO EAT TURNIPS TO SURVIVE!...

AS GOD IS IN HEAVEN AND DONALD TRUMP IS MY NAME...

HINT: CLARK GABLE, VIVIEN LEIGH...

...I'LL NEVER BE POOR AGAIN!

NO, NOT "FLUBBER."

FIRST, I'LL PUT TOGETHER AN AUTO-FACTORY DEAL... WE'LL MAKE...

TRUMP-PRINCESS II

..."COUP DE TRUMPS."

THEN MAYBE A RESTAURANT...

...SERVING RUMP ROAST OF TRUMP.

AND A SOUP COMPANY! "TRUMP SOUP"!...

FEATURING "CHICKEN 'N' TRUMPLINGS."

MAYBE IT'S TIME WE RECONSIDER COMMUNISM.

TRUMP PRINCESS

DONALD... I HAVE A CONFESSION TO MAKE.

YES, MY LITTLE ONYX PEA?

I LIQUIDATED OUR BILLIONS AND REDEDICATED MY LIFE TO EASING THE SUFFERING OF STARVING THIRD-WORLD CHILDREN.

I'M KIDDING, YOU BIG GULUMP.

DON'T DO THAT, IVANA!

A THOUSAND POINTS OF LIGHT.

SO VERY FAR ABOVE ME,

WHAT SECRETS DO YOU HOLD?

T... R... U... M... P...

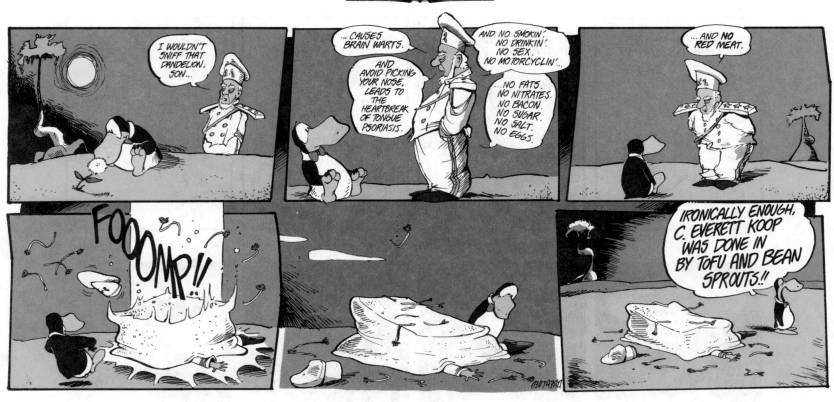

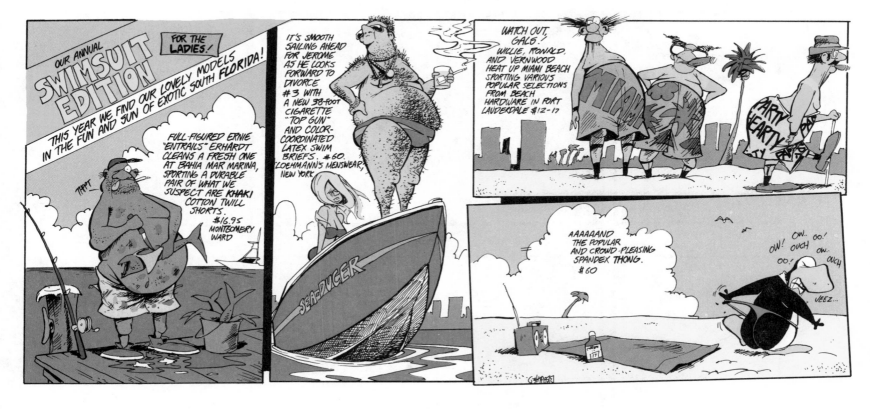

..DON'T FORGET TO WEAR YOUR RUBBERS ON RAINY DAYS!

OKAY.

AND MARRY A NICE PLAIN GIRL NAMED "MEG" OR "CINDY." ...IF SHE'S BEAUTIFUL, SHE'LL ONLY BREAK YOUR HEART.

SIX MINUTES: $8.25. VISA OR MASTERCARD?

"DIAL-A-MOM."

..AND STOP SLOUCHING, SON... NICE GIRLS AREN'T ATTRACTED TO BAD POSTURE.

MOM, GET OUT OF MY LIFE, YOU NARROW-MINDED, MEDDLING BUSY-BODY!!

OKAY, BUT ALWAYS KNOW THAT I WOULD GLADLY RIP BOTH MY LEGS OFF AND FEED THEM TO CROCODILES TO SAVE YOUR LIFE.

GOD, HOW I NEED TO HEAR THAT NOW AND THEN.

...NINE MINUTES: $12.75...

OO... YOUR MANLY VOICE MAKES ME SO... WARM. ARE YOU GETTING WARM?

IT'S ONLY APRIL.

I'M TAKING OFF SOME PIECES OF CLOTHING... WANT ME TO DESCRIBE THEM?

NO.

WHAT DO YOU WANT ME TO CALL YOU? I KNOW! "TIGER"!

I FIGURE I MISDIALED "DIAL-A-MOM." WHADYA THINK?

YOU CAN CALL ME "D. LISHUS THIGH"...

PHONE BILL'S HERE!

UH-OH.

ONE CALL TO DUBUQUE... ONE TO MADISON...

HOLD IT...

374 CALLS TO SOMEWHERE NEAR HOBOKEN.

NO...

$6,392.24.

I WONDER IF PETE ROSE'S STOMACH FELT LIKE THIS?

WHAT?! NO BRAN MUFFINS?!

I EAT OAT BRAN EVERY DAY!

...LIKE EVERY OTHER KINDA COOL, LATE-EIGHTIES QUALITY DUDE!

WHAT?! NO BRAN SCUM?!

MEANWHILE...BACK AT TRUMP'S BRAIN...

IVANA! IT'S ME!!

SELL THE JUNK, IVANA! BOATS... CASTLES... JETS... SELL ALL THE TOYS!!

LET'S FEED AFRICA FOR TWENTY YEARS!

...JUUUUST KIDDING.

I KNEW IT.

OH, PLEASE! LET'S GO OVER IT ALL JUST ONE MORE TIME!

TRUMP TOWERS... THE TRUMP PLAZA...THE TRUMP CASTLE... TRUMP AIRLINES... TRUMP ESTATES... AND THE "TRUMP PRINCESS"!

WHO ARE YOU TALKING TO?

THE TRUMP FRUMP.

IVANA!

COME AGAIN?

NOTHING, MY TULIP!

A SIXTEEN-PAGE AUTOBIOGRAPHY? I HOPE YOU AT LEAST TOLD ABOUT THAT SPECIAL SUMMER...

..THE SUMMER WHEN LIFE AND LOVE SEEMED ONLY A SIGH APART...WHEN THE FUTURE LAY PRONE BEFORE YOU...LIKE A WOMAN... BEGUILING... SEDUCTIVE...

...ETERNAL.

I TOLD ABOUT THAT JULY I BELCHED DURING "MOONSTRUCK."

YES. GOOD.

PLEASE LIMIT MINDLESS BLATHER WITH AUTHOR TO 30 SECONDS

"A PENGUIN'S STORY"

"A PENGUIN'S STORY"

"A PENGUIN'S STORY"

MILO SAID THAT AT LEAST THIS ISN'T AS BAD AS HAVING MY EYEBALLS SKEWERED BY RED-HOT POKERS COVERED WITH ANTS.

BUT I'M NOT SURE.

"A PENG..."

HOW COULD NOBODY SHOW UP FOR MY AUTOGRAPH PARTY ?! NOBODY !

"A FEW UNSOLD COPIES"

HOLD IT...YOU DIDN'T SEE THAT COCKROACH THAT SHOWED UP EARLY ON ?

SURE.

WELL, THERE YA GO ! A CUSTOMER ! WHERE IS HE ?

RIGHT HERE.

HOW CAN YOU WALK ALL OVER YOUR FANS LIKE THAT ?

I'M REWRITING YOUR AUTOBIOGRAPHY. I NEED TO CONFIRM SOME NEW MATERIAL...

I HEARD YOU AND JACK KENNEDY PLAYED "HIDE THE GUACAMOLE" WITH 19 ROCKETTES DURING INAUGURATION NIGHT.

DID THAT HAPPEN ?

WELL, YEAH... IN A DREAM I HAD AFTER A MEAL OF BAD ENCHILADAS...

BUT IN A SENSE, IT DID HAPPEN ?

WELL, YEAH... BUT—

THE "WASHINGTON POST" WORKS THIS WAY, OF COURSE.

I MUST SAY... I'M FEELING QUITE SECURE LATELY.

AS IF I'VE FINALLY FOUND MY NICHE...

HERE. IN BLOOM COUNTY... I FEEL A REAL SENSE OF...

...PERMANENCE.

DABBLING IN A BIT OF IRONIC FORESHADOWING, ARE WE ?

NO... WHY ?

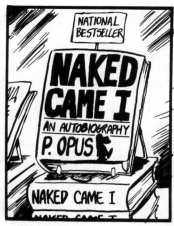

MILO! IT'S "PEOPLE" MAGAZINE! THEY WANNA KNOW MORE ABOUT THAT RIDICULOUS CHAPTER ABOUT ME AND THE 247 STARLETS IN CANNES! SET THE RECORD STRAIGHT!!

I'M MR. OPUS'S GHOSTWRITER. ALL THAT CANNES STUFF WAS A TYPO.

NO. HE NEVER SEDUCED ANY 247 GORGEOUS STARLETS... NO. OF COURSE NOT. RIDICULOUS. LAUGHABLE...

...RIGHT. NOT ONE.

MAYBE ONE.

DON'T GET MAD. I JUST SOLD THE TELEVISION RIGHTS TO "NAKED CAME I." FILMING STARTS MONDAY.

YOU'VE RUINED MY LIFE! DO YOU UNDERSTAND? RUINED!

WHO'LL BE PLAYING—?

GARY COLEMAN WITH A PUTTY NOSE.

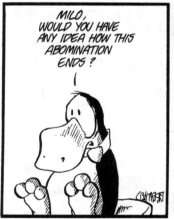

I'M WATCHING GARY COLEMAN PLAY OUT MY LIFE IN "NAKED CAME I: THE TV MOVIE."

MILO, WOULD YOU HAVE ANY IDEA HOW THIS ABOMINATION ENDS?

YEAH. HE ENDS UP WATCHING HIS LIFE LIBELED IN FRONT OF MILLIONS, SO HE GRABS A BAZOOKA AND GOES AFTER THE GUY PLAYING ME.

SWEPT HELPLESSLY ALONG BY THE TIDE OF HISTORY!

KIDS! YESTERDAY, YOU SAW ME SITTING THIS CLOSE TO THE TELEVISION SCREEN.

DON'T TRY THAT YOURSELVES! AS YOUR PARENTS CAN EXPLAIN, THE FOLLOWING CAN EASILY HAPPEN:

PHEWPPPPT...

SO BE CAREFUL!

PLUS, DON'T CHASE PEOPLE WITH BAZOOKAS.

PUBLIC SERVICE MESSAGE

LOLA! LOLA LOLA GRANOLA!

HI, SWEETIE!

EL BLOB-BUTT'S EX-FIANCÉE!

SO! WHAT HAVE YOU GOT PLANNED AFTER THIS GIG CLOSES?

"PLAYBOY" WANTS TO FEATURE ME EXPOSING MYSELF!

THEY PROMISED THAT EVERY MECHANIC IN AMERICA WOULD BE SLOBBERING AT MY BODY BY CHRISTMAS! SO GUESS WHAT?...

YOUR BRAIN TURNED TO CLAM SAUCE AND YOU SAID YES.

"CHASE YOUR DREAMS", I ALWAYS SAY!

FAREWELL, MILO! BYE, BINKLEY! SO LONG, LOLA!

SEE YOU LATER, BILL THE CAT!

GOOD LUCK

TOODLE-OO, STEVE AND CUTTER JOHN! TATA, PORTNOY, HODGE, OLIVER!

ADIOS, FRIENDS! AU REVOIR, FAMILY! ARRIVEDERCI, EVERYONE!...

GOOD-BYE, ME.

ALONE.

NOBODY LEFT.

I'M ON MY OWN.

...WITH MY OWN RULES.

FER INSTANCE, I CAN WAD MY UNDERWEAR INTO TINY BALLS, AND NO ONE WILL NAG ME!

I CAN TRACK MUD IN WHEN IT RAINS!

I'M GUARANTEED IMMUNITY!

I CAN SNORT AND SWEAR AND BELCH...

...AND PICK YOUR NOSE WITH IMPUNITY!

YAAA!

DID I STARTLE YOU, OPUS?

NO! NO, I ALWAYS MOUSSE MY HAIR LIKE THIS... JEEZ.

PANT PANT

I THOUGHT I WAS ALONE..

NAW! NO ONE HAS TO BE ALONE... I'LL SHOW YOU!

WE'RE GOING OVER TO THE WRONG SIDE OF THE TRACKS?

I LIVE HERE.

RIGHT SIDE

WRONG SIDE

ANY WAY OUT?

FUNNY YOU SHOULD MENTION "OUT"...

HOTEL